D1450803

NAHC
Hunting Camp Lore

North American Hunting Club
Minnetonka, Minnesota

Mike Vail
Vice President, Products and Business Development

Tom Carpenter
Director of Book and New Media Development

Mike Faw
Editor

Dan Kennedy
Book Production Manager

Heather Koshiol
Book Development Coordinator

Zins Design Studio
Book Design and Production
  Scott Zins
  Ingrid Lang

ISBN 1-58159-023-7
1 2 3 4 5 6 7 8 9 10

PHOTO CREDITS – Cover onlay (clockwise from left): Bill Marchel, Michael D. Faw, Lon E. Lauber, Phil Aarrestad.
Line art illustrations by Larry Anderson unless otherwise noted.

CONTENTS

Introduction

Bill Miller, Executive Director—
North American Hunting Club.

Members of the North American Hunting Club consistently tell us that their favorite benefit of membership is *North American Hunter.* Having worked on that magazine for nearly 15 years now, makes me feel mighty good. The NAHC's growth from 75,000 to 750,000 members, along with the ever-improving quality of the Club's publications, rival the trophies I have on the wall as a source of pride.

But it's not just the work of a crackerjack staff that makes NAHC publications highly lauded by Club members. Equally important are the things that make our magazines and books different from those you'd pick up on the newsstand or in the bookstore. NAHC publications are largely by Club members for Club members. The Club's publications aren't the theories and pompocities of a bunch of editors with offices in New York City. The NAHC's stories are about, by and for real hunters, hunters who spend upward of 30, 40 or 50 days in the woods each year. The "pros" you read in the magazines and books are Club members, too, so they view the "readers" as "fellow members"...as equals.

Nowhere is this more evident than in *Hunting Camp Lore*. This outstanding book compiles great hunting stories, invaluable hunting tips and one-of-a-kind hunting facts lived, learned and contributed by North American Hunting Club members. Sure, you'll see sections by "big name" outdoor professionals like Larry Weishuhn pop up here and there. But as well-known and widely traveled as "Mr. Whitetail" is, rest assured he's a "fellow member" and regular guy at heart. Larry loves to hear a fellow member's hunting tale as much or more than he likes to tell one.

- You'll find some of Larry's advice, and tons of other stories and lore, in the book's first section: *A Passion for Deer Hunting*. We know what makes our members tick, and deer hunting is the name of the game. These adventures and strategies are sure to entertain and enlighten.

- Then, we'll take you beyond whitetail country and after elk, muleys, pronghorns, bears and other North American favorites in *The Adventure of Big Game*. If you've hunted any of this game before, you'll love this section; if you haven't, your appetite will certainly be whetted, your knowledge expanded.

- Many of us are becoming addicted to a new type of hunting, one that combines the challenge of big game hunting with a wily bird that is continually expanding its range. *Big Game Birds: Wild Turkey* is certain to teach you some new techniques and tricks while taking you right out to the turkey woods for a spring or fall adventure.

- To finish up, we bring you *Essential Tips, Lists & Other Lore* — a veritable grab bag of information you'll need, no matter what type of hunting you're planning.

Hunting Camp Lore is a book of many purposes. It's a book to help you enjoy more success in your own hunting. It's a book to give you the edge when a hunting camp "philosophical" debate erupts. It's a book to expand your hunting knowledge by challenging that which you accept as "fact." But more than anything else, it's a book to allow you to celebrate in the successes of your fellow members and to remind you of "the best part" of being a North American Hunting Club member.

Enjoy *"Hunting Camp Lore."* And enjoy your membership in the NAHC.

Bill Miller

Bill Miller
Executive Director

A PASSION FOR DEER HUNTING

Sometimes, as a hunter, you have to pass along the tradition. Finding the right student to share your hunting skills and secret hunting places with can be a challenge, especially if the student is a bit on the lazy side. Some hunters go to great extremes to introduce a kid to hunting and the outdoors.

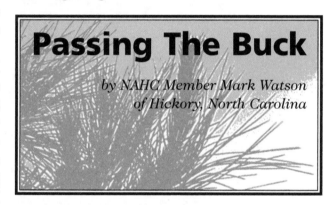

Passing The Buck

*by NAHC Member Mark Watson
of Hickory, North Carolina*

Here's what I mean. I scouted a great deer hunting place near my home several week-ends before the whitetail hunting season opened. I kept seeing a nice seven-pointer in one certain area about 9:00 a.m. on each scouting trip. The buck, and a lot of does, liked to bed on a south ridge near some big white oak trees. The steep terrain and plentiful food made this a real deer paradise. I killed four bucks there one season from the same treestand as the deer came to eat acorns.

This hunting season I decided to ask a new kid in the neighborhood if he wanted to deer hunt with me. He responded "yes." But I never could get him up early on the weekends to go scouting because he liked to sleep in late. Finally, deer season arrived and I told him I was going hunting. He said he was ready and had all of his equipment. I discovered that all the deer hunting equipment he had was a rifle, so I loaned him the rest of what he would need, including a knife, treestand steps and a safety belt.

Next, I told him I had a great place for him to hunt. I was going to let him hunt the buck. When I said that we needed to go hang a treestand for him to hunt from, he was eager to go. Unfortunately, he gave out before we completed the hike to the top of the mountain. I had to carry the treestand that I loaned to him the rest of the way to the top of the mountain.

When we arrived at the site I had chosen for his stand, I began to show him the numerous deer trails, scrapes and rubs. He just sat on the ground and looked around. I then suggested that he look at a few of the nearby trees and pick one to hang the stand in. He continued just sitting on the ground and looking around. When I asked what was wrong, he replied that he was still tired from the hike up the mountain. I screwed in the steps and hung the treestand while he watched.

Then I showed him how to use the safety belt and had him climb up in the stand. I told him to look to the west. Along the old logging trail he was looking down on was where I had often seen the buck traveling, and the trail was only 30 yards away from the stand. I told him I normally saw the buck before 9:00 a.m. so he should stay alert. I explained where my treestand was on another ridge——across a nearby field and about a quarter mile away from where he would be hunting. We then returned home, but I sensed he was afraid to be in the woods by himself. I told him I was close by and could hear him if he shouted and needed help.

The next day we arrived at the field well before daylight, and I sent the young hunter to his end of the field and toward the treestand. Up to this point I had done everything for him, now all he had to do was sit there and shoot a buck. I went on to my stand and settled in to hunt.

Around 9:00 a.m. I heard three shots from over at the new apprentice hunter's stand. He had never really been deer hunting before this day, and I had tried to teach him many of the better tips, but his laziness had frequently overcome his desire to hunt.

A few minutes after the shots rang out, I saw him dash into the field and run toward me. He was moving faster than I had ever seen him move, and, oddly enough, he did not have a coat or a shirt on. The air temperature was well below freezing, and the novice had stripped down to just his T-shirt. I found this very odd, not to mention that he was flashing a lot of white as he dashed across that ridge-top field.

When the novice hunter sprinted up to the base of the tree I was perched in, he blurted out something with the word I thought indicated

NAHC Member Jake Wheeler of Morganton, North Carolina, overcame his lackluster days as a beginning deer hunter and now hunts whitetails across North America.

"got" in the sentence. He was out of breath and overcome with the cold or excitement. I was not sure which one of those factors had the best of him, but I climbed down, pulled my coat off and handed it to him. When the novice warmed up, I determined he had indeed shot a buck and that I was needed to help field dress the animal. I packed up my gear and said I would go help him.

We strolled back across the field and entered the woods and walked down the ridge to the treestand I had loaned him. His excitement had waned enough that he was now speaking understandably. I stood there looking around but did not see a deer. The novice was digging through his pack for the knife. When he found the knife, he stood up and stared at me oddly. I could tell he was waiting for me to do something by the expression on his face. He finally stated that he wanted me to field dress his deer.

I told him that we could not field dress a deer that I could not see. I asked where the deer was and did he actually see it fall down and stay. Finally, the novice calmed down enough to tell me the deer was dead and that he had covered it up with his shirt and coat. That explained why he was missing the clothing. But where was the deer? The novice pointed south and I walked over to where he had pointed but did not see the deer.

When I paused and looked back, the novice pointed in another direction. This was enough cat and mouse for me so I had him climb up in the stand and point to where the deer was standing when he shot it. I soon saw scuffed hoof prints in the soil and followed drops of blood across a small distant ridge. I located the deer and determined the antlered buck was the same one I had seen on my scouting trips to the area. The buck was lying hidden under the novice hunter's shirt, hunting coat and a pile of leaves. The apprentice hunter told me that he was afraid someone would find his buck and steal it, something I had never considered in my country neighborhood.

Next I guided him through the field dressing process and helped drag the buck to my jeep. I was happy that he had gotten his first deer and that the hunt had turned out so well, even though this hunt had required a lot of extra work on my part. However, I was speechless when the novice commented, "You sure don't know much about deer. You said this buck would be there by 9:00 a.m. and my watch read 9:05 a.m. when I first saw the deer."

Fortunately, he grew out of his laziness and became an industrious individual. We have since gone on numerous hunts together, and he always carries more than his share of responsibility. His early hunting days sure had me worried, though!

What else could go wrong today? We got up late and missed our chance to go with five other guys on a deer drive. After two years of no luck, I figured that this was a sign. I mean, who could go home empty-handed on a deer drive in Iowa? It seems as though the only people who get deer in Iowa are those who participate in a drive. I now know that isn't the whole truth, but for us who are still new in the hunting game, it definitely increases our chances.

Sometimes, Luck Is All You Need

by NAHC Life Member Randy Hutson
of Iowa City, Iowa

Well, after missing the deer drive, my son and I decided to catch some more shut-eye. Opening day is always a day to be excited about, but my plans had already gone bad. When plan number one goes wrong, a guy has to have a plan number two. Since I work two jobs averaging 80 hours a week, more sleep is always something that is on my mind. My second plan was to get all the rest I needed and then go out to the public property and hunt with the rest of the county.

It was close to noon when my son and I left the house. As we pulled out on the highway, I remember thinking, "Why am I going out this late? My chances have already been lowered by missing my deer drive, and I haven't even been out to scout in this area this year." My spirits were a little low, but there was an underlying excitement knowing that the season I loved so much had finally arrived.

Looking back now, I am so glad I did go. Sometimes a little luck is all you need. I not only got a deer, but this buck has 11 points on his magnificent rack and he looks very impressive hanging on my wall.

It all started eight years ago when my Grampa died and left me his Marlin .22 caliber lever-action rifle. I had only been out with Grampa and Dad on three occasions to hunt during my childhood, but I always loved every moment of it—out with the men for a day of fun and unforeseen adventure. Just to walk through the woods and walk on ground I had never seen before was an adventure on its own. I have always loved the outdoors. The trees, streams, rolling hills and fresh air of the country have always excited me.

After Gramma gave Grampa's rifle to me, I started spending a lot of time out shooting. Soon I began to purchase other guns. Each time I would want to purchase a gun, my wife would ask me what I would do with the gun and why did I feel like I had to have it. For the first couple of guns, I explained to her that I liked to target practice and just plain enjoyed shooting each of them. It soon became obvious to me that my excuses for buying guns would come to an abrupt end without warning if I didn't figure out something to do with them that made them a useful tool. It was at that point that I decided I would give hunting a chance again.

My experience at hunting was very limited. I was completely unaware of the love for hunting that was deep within me just waiting to be unleashed. After I decided to take up hunting, I found myself buying all the reading material available to me and becoming consumed with my new passion. For months I spent all my spare time studying guns and reading stories about all kinds of hunts. I found myself falling into an irreversible love for hunting deer, moose, elk and bear. Someday, I will be able to say I've hunted each. I've never been sorry for opening my life to hunting. In fact, it has been one of the most satisfying hobbies I've ever started.

NAHC Life Member Randy Hutson of Iowa City, Iowa, proudly displays the 11-point white-tailed buck he bagged while hunting with his son, Brian.

I think the most exciting thing about hunting is all the strategy involved. I would have never guessed how hard it is to learn all the habits and behaviors of game animals. My only regret is that I waited so long to find this new love. The gratification it brings to me to be able to provide meat for the table has been enlightening.

And enlightening it was this first Saturday of the second shotgun season. My son and I arrived at the public property at 1:00 p.m. We drove around the property for some time before we arrived at our final destination. We talked about going to the spot where we had hunted last year. We knew there were deer there. We had seen many there in the previous years; however, we had only seen does and hadn't been lucky enough to see a buck there yet. Oh, you always know they are there somewhere, but until you become smarter than they are, you don't get to witness their presence even though their sign is everywhere.

This year, though, we decided to go toward the back of the property, stay with the wind in our faces and see if our luck would be any different. As we reached the parking lot at the back of the property, we noticed a large number of cars, trucks and vans already there. We decided there were too many vehicles for us, so we went on down the road about a mile and found another parking lot with no vehicles there. This looked promising—no other hunters to contend with and perfect deer country to hunt in.

It was a beautiful day to hunt. The temperature was about 35 degrees, and the wind was out of the northwest at maybe five or ten miles per hour. At 1:00 in the afternoon, the sun made the snow look majestic, like a carpet lying in the woods. The afternoon shadows of the bare trees made a mystic scene on the snow. The air was crisp and the sound of gunfire to our right indicated that our neighbors were successful in their quest for the elusive deer.

As my son and I walked into the woods, I retold him a story I had recently heard on the evening news about a man in his middle 60s who was explaining to a news correspondent his approach to hunting white-tailed deer. He prided himself on the fact that he no longer went on long hikes into the woods and still came back with his buck. He told the reporter that he now only went into the woods about a quarter to a half mile and would then just sit and wait for an hour or two until his buck showed up. He bragged that he had never gone home empty-handed. The deer the hunter presented in the news story was indeed a beauty of a buck.

After telling my son this story, I asked his opinion about giving it a try. I think both of us had little hope of even seeing a deer that day, so any method seemed okay at the time. As we entered the woods, we noticed a tree that had a lot of branches hanging down from it. The tree also had a branch that had fallen next to it, making a nice gun rest. We moved to that tree and noticed that ahead of us about 25 yards was a deer trail. This tree was perfect for the two of us, providing protection from the wind and excellent concealment. We had only been there five minutes when I heard several deer run in behind us.

Just prior to these deer appearing, there had been a barrage of gunfire over to the right where all the vehicles had been. It was easy to figure that the hunters who were east of us had literally chased these deer over to us. When the deer reached our footprints in the snow where we had entered the woods, they all came to an abrupt stop.

Our scent had obviously piqued their attention. Danger was near again, and the deer knew it. As I looked around the tree, my heart rate started to climb. I was astonished to see a group of five deer only 40 yards behind me. They didn't know we were there because we were on the north side of the tree looking into the wind. They only knew our scent was there and that was enough to make them very jittery. I guess it was just instinct, but immediately I took aim on the deer in the middle. As I started to pull the trigger of my shotgun, I was elated to realize that the deer I was aiming at was the buck among four does. As I took aim with my open-sighted slug barrel shotgun, I remembered proclaiming to my son, "It's a buck!" Then the shotgun roared.

Brian must have been daydreaming or something, because he knew nothing of what was going on until I pulled the trigger. As soon as he heard the shot, he jumped to his feet, saw the buck stagger backward and started to run for him. "Wait!" I whispered rather loudly. "Let him die before we go after him."

After watching the deer try to escape for only 20 yards, the buck dropped with all his limbs tucked neatly under his body and with his head dropped as if to take a nap. It was over. My deer season only lasted 25 minutes. It may have been quick, but those 25 minutes will be a lasting memory that my son and I will share forever. Brian and I were like two little kids all the way home. We both knew that Mom would never believe our catch. She didn't until she saw him in the back of the truck.

My son and I can hardly wait until next year so we can try it again. And next year, he will get to hunt with me since he will turn 16. Maybe next year we'll have a little luck again. We both know that more skill will come in time and with practice. Right now, we're both just happy to be learning and hunting.

Deer Hunting Tips from the Pros

- To determine whether a set of deer tracks was left by a buck or a doe, remember that:

  —A buck's stride will be longer than a doe's.

  —A large buck, with its long, bull-legged gait, will leave a wide set of tracks. A doe will tend to walk with one foot directly in front of the other, keeping its tracks almost in a straight line.

  —The larger the buck, the wider and deeper the imprint in the back part of the track.

  —A buck will often drag its feet.

  —When hunting a buck, keep your eyes open for signs of feeding. After browsing, rutting bucks will usually bed down nearby.

- Deer tend to travel and feed more during a full moon. If hunting during a full moon, make an effort to hunt during midday since the deer will be more active.

- Deer tend to browse more prior to a rainstorm. If hunting during an approaching rainstorm, hunt as long as safely possible.

- Keep your deer hunting clothing as scent-free as possible. With your clothing, mix some of the cover you will be hunting in, such as pine boughs.

- The state game department can tell you the primary peak rut for your area. After you determine that, count 25 days forward to determine the secondary rut period. If the does haven't been impregnated, this is the time when they will again come back into estrus.

W hite-tailed deer have been my vocation for over thirty years, having entered the wildlife biologist field back in 1969. Whitetails have always been one of my passions. They were the reason I wanted to be a wildlife biologist. They were also the primary reason I wanted to be an outdoor writer. I owe the white-tailed deer—plenty!

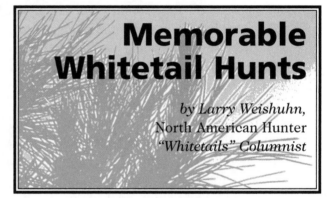

Memorable Whitetail Hunts

by Larry Weishuhn,
North American Hunter
"Whitetails" Columnist

Mounts of numerous fine bucks I have taken throughout their range in North America decorate my office wall. Not only do I enjoy looking at the mounts, I view them as a tribute to the deer I hunted. Each mount helps me to intimately recall every detail that went into their hunting and taking.

There have been many memorable bucks, but without a doubt, the most memorable is my first, taken in Colorado County, Texas, where I grew up. My dad, mom and I hunted about a mile west of our house on property that belonged to our neighbors. We earned hunting permission by helping them work cattle and hauling hay. Throughout the summer, I lived in those woods, scouting for deer, or so I am sure it seemed to my parents. That year I chose to hunt with an old single-barrel 12 gauge shotgun that had belonged to my maternal grandfather. Finally, the first morning of the 1961 hunting season arrived. The gray early light had just started getting bright enough to see the floor of the woods around me from my perch high in an old oak tree when the first shot of the season sounded. I gripped the old 12 gauge tightly, sure that this would be the day I would finally take a deer.

Moments later I heard the telltale hoof falls of a deer walking on dry oak leaves. I turned in the direction of the sound and saw a small buck, less than 20 yards away. Immediately, buck fever set in. I was shaking terribly as I raised the old shotgun. I more or less put the front bead in the notch of the receiver with the barrel pointed at the deer's shoulder, cocked the hammer and pulled the trigger.

At the shot, the young buck fell to the ground but immediately was up and moving. I hurriedly broke open the single barrel shotgun and, in the process, pulled the forearm off of the barrel, which in turn disengaged the barrel from the receiver. The barrel fell to the ground, landing with a "thud" as it stuck in the soft soil below the tree. There I sat, the buttstock and receiver in one hand and the forearm in the other and the barrel stuck in the ground 30 feet below.

I was frantic! My deer gun was in pieces, my deer was running away and I didn't know what to do. Finally, less than five seconds later (although at the time it seemed like an eternity), I regained my composure, stuck the two major gun parts I held in my hands into my hunting vest and crawled down the tree. On the ground, I cleaned the sand out of the barrel, reassembled my gun, loaded it and headed to where I had last seen my buck disappear.

Thankfully the Number 4 buckshot had done its job and the little buck had scarcely run more than 30 yards. While looking for the deer I nearly stepped on it. A few extremely rapid heart beats later, the realization hit me: not only was I a deer hunter, now I was a successful deer hunter! Although they never admitted it, I suspect my parents were concerned (not knowing what was happening) when they heard me whoop and holler for joy. Even now, these many years later, it seems as if that major event in my life happened only this morning!

First deer are important. When I was growing up in the 1950s and early '60s, taking your first buck was considered a rite of passage to adulthood. Though times may have changed a bit, first deer are definitely a milestone in any hunter's life, whether he or she started hunting as a youngster or not until well into the adult years.

Another of my most memorable hunts in- volves hunting with my two daughters, Theresa and Beth. Each shot their first deer when they were eight years old. I strongly believe we need to start children hunting very early in life, teaching them how to shoot along with the responsibilities that come with guns and hunting.

Both of my daughters shot their first deer under very similar circum-

Author Larry Weishuhn has turned his interest in deer and hunting into a career.

stances. We hunted out of comfortable blinds, where they were protected from the cold and the elements. In those blinds, there was no telling how many chocolate chip cookies, peanuts, chips and snack foods we ate and how many gallons of hot chocolate we drank. I wanted hunting to be a fun experience for them. Both were taught how to shoot early in their young lives and where to hit a deer when a shot was taken in order to kill the animal as quickly and humanely as possible.

I also waited for just the right animal to come along before allowing them to take a shot. The prerequisite was it had to be a small-racked buck. I did not want them taking a big buck for their first deer. Big bucks should only come along after years of hunting and learning to appreciate what goes into the making of a big-racked mature buck.

When the "right deer" appeared, I would ease my Ruger—shortened to their length of pull stock and chambered in 7 X 57 Mauser—toward the deer. Then I'd turn over the scoped rifle to one of my daughters. In each instance, the same thing happened. As one of my daughters prepared to shoot, I would watch the deer through a binocular to see where the bullet would strike. Without realizing it, I would catch a severe case of buck fever and begin breathing very quickly, deeply and erratically. The next thing I'd know, one of my very concerned daughters would be tugging on my shirt sleeve, questioning, "Daddy, Daddy! Are you all right? Are you having a heart attack?"

Then I would realize what I was doing, calm down and assure the respective daughter that I was fine, just a bit excited. Satisfied about her dad's condition, each daughter carefully aimed and squeezed the trigger, killing the deer instantly in its tracks. Full-blown buck fever wouldn't set in until we approached the downed deer.

That's what hunting is all about! Hunting whitetails is supposed to be fun and exciting. It is always rewarding!

One of my favorite whitetails is one I referred to for five years as "Ol' Tobe." I first saw Tobe while doing a helicopter survey on a South Texas ranch. He was an absolute monster, 12 typical points, with a long drop-tine off both main beams and a 26- to 28-inch-wide outside spread. He was the kind of buck I dream about. I dubbed him "Tobe" the third year I hunted him. Although I only saw him the one time out of the helicopter, ranch hands kept me informed of his antler status. He seemed to remain the same each year, not unlike an old man who lived down the road from us when I was growing up. His name was Tobe.

Thankfully, I had permission to hunt the ranch. For the next five years I hunted Tobe, yet I never saw him. Had it not been for ranch hands telling about occasionally seeing him, I would have assumed he had been killed by lions or coyotes.

Finally, six years after I had first seen him, I walked up on an ancient-looking buck walking a trail behind the dam of a waterhole. He moved like a 90-year-old man and had about the same muscle tone, but on his head he wore an extremely fine rack. That's when I saw something that appeared to be hanging off of his right main beam.

Quickly, I drew my rifle to my shoulder, peered through the scope and confirmed he had at least one drop-tine. That was all it took, and when the crosshairs settled on the deer's shoulder, I squeezed the trigger. Moments later, I stood admiring a buck with 18 total points—each point more than an inch long—with a 23-inch outside spread and three drop-tines. A quick check in his mouth revealed the absence of nearly all his teeth. Could it be? It had to be Tobe ... it was!

Which is my favorite whitetail hunt? Why, of course, the next one I go on.

What Is Choke in a Shotgun Barrel?

Shotgun barrels originated in the early 16th century and remained remarkably the same for nearly 300 years. They were basically straight tubes that produced unpredictable patterns and were effective for very short range. The only means of extending the effective range was by adding more shot.

It wasn't until the middle of the 1800s that someone found that a slight constriction at the muzzle tightened the pattern considerably and increased the shotgunner's options. The shot charge was constricted or "choked" as it left the barrel, and the effect is dramatic.

"Through the years, gunmakers found that barrels could only be constricted a maximum of about .040 inch before things became too crowded and the pattern started to deteriorate," says shooting expert Frank Ventimiglia, vice president of Shooter's Choice gun care products. "That's what was termed full choke. The industry standard for full choke was that it would put 70 percent of the pellets in its pattern within a 30-inch circle at 40 yards.

"Today, of course, guns can pattern much denser than 70 percent even though they aren't necessarily choked any tighter. Some turkey guns put all of their pellets in the circle—100 percent at 40 yards. But that's more a function of shotgun shell design. The introduction of plastic shotcups, harder shot and buffering has so improved shotshells that old standards no longer apply."

Source: Shooter's Choice

White-Tailed Deer Facts

A deer snorts by a violent expulsion of air through the nostrils while keeping its mouth closed.

The thumping foot-stomp is the only non-vocal sound a deer makes.

Does have been known to rear on their back legs and strike at each other with their front legs and hooves—much like boxers in a ring.

By the time a fawn is one month old, all nursing has normally stopped. Does normally kick strange fawns away when they try to nurse.

A fawn can stand upright within 15 minutes after being born.

Bucks can become locked together while fighting. The deer can die of wounds, exhaustion or the inability to eat or drink.

Direct eye contact is seen as a sign of aggression among deer. Bucks will rarely face each other or bed facing each other.

A melanistic, excessively dark colored white-tailed deer is very rare.

The velvet that covers a buck's growing antlers is full of blood vessels and nerves. A buck takes great care to protect the antlers and to avoid pain or wounds that can lead to infections.

I had barely hung up my rattling antlers and picked my bow off its perch when I heard a faint crunch in the distance. When a twig snapped, I pinpointed the location and caught my first glimpse of antler. It was he, the mysterious deer nicknamed "the ghost buck" by local hunters. My pulse began to race.

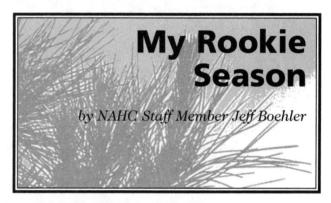

My Rookie Season

by NAHC Staff Member Jeff Boehler

Luckily, I was up in my treestand at 18 feet with the buck upwind, so I didn't think scent was a problem. Still over 40 yards away, the buck stepped behind a gnarled tangle of brush. I could hear my heart pound as I quietly and mechanically tried to slip an arrow from my quiver. I cringed as the arrow made a "twang" when it was released by the quiver. Miraculously, the buck didn't notice the sound, and I slowly lowered the arrow onto my bow. I froze as the buck stepped into the open and continued down the trail toward me.

I only had one chance, and as the buck stepped behind another patch of brush, I drew back and held steady. When this beast moved into the shooting lane, I carefully placed the bow's bright red sight pin just behind his shoulder and began squeezing the release... beep... beep... beep. What was that horrible noise and

Illustration by Jeff Boehler

why now? Beep... beep. I raised my arm and slapped the alarm. Wow, what a dream! I began to emerge from a deep sleep and turned on the light. The time was 4:30 a.m... on the opening day of bow season.

I drove west in the dark, sipping coffee and listening to the radio. I know every mile of this road through the rolling farm country as if it were just another cul-de-sac in my own neighborhood. I had hung a stand in a relative's woodlot not far from our duck blinds. Last year we found fresh sign of a big buck taking sanctuary in these woods, maybe the buck—the "ghost buck." Even though last year's adjacent cornfield was now planted in beans, I had hopes that this local legend was still hanging around.

The ghost buck is a monstrous beast that has been sighted on numerous occasions, but rarely through the crosshairs of a scope. It's seen after deer season, or maybe before, but seldom during. My father-in-law saw it after the close of last season and said it more resembled a small cow with massive antlers than a whitetail. Bob, our lifelong friend who owns the land where we duck hunt, got the closest view of the deer a couple of years ago. Normally an excellent shot, Bob was still hunting the creek behind his farm when the ghost buck sprang from its bed, just a handful of paces away. Five quick shots at the running giant and not touching a hair on its body only added fuel to the fire that it is indeed a ghost.

I had been looking forward to this opening day of bowhunting season for a year and a half. I outfitted my bow well before last year's hunting season and practiced often. But the luck of drawing a bear tag and elk tag made for a busy fall. Coupled with a banner year for ducks and geese in our neck of the woods, there was little time for bowhunting. The bow season came and went without me ever hanging a stand.

Determined to become a bowhunter this season, I practiced all summer. In August, I started shooting at the 3-D deer target my thoughtful and understanding wife had given me for my birthday. I didn't apply for a western hunt, didn't draw a bear tag and was committed to spending more time in the woods learning about the crafty whitetail. I had high hopes for my rookie bowhunting season.

The season was about to start, and already the odds were not in my favor. I cursed the weather channel as I pulled into the farmyard and noticed the wind was from the south, not the northeast wind they had promised me an hour ago on TV. I had really been counting on the prevailing north wind when I hung my stand at the southern edge of the woodlot. Now the wind would blow my scent northward, toward the trail any respectable deer would use. But I woke up too early, drove too far and was too excited to turn around and go home now. I was going hunting—wind or no wind.

After going through the new routine of getting all my paraphernalia strapped on, I tiptoed down the trail and shimmied up the tree. Then came the balancing act of attaching the safety strap to the tree, pulling up my bow, securing the quiver, hanging my fanny pack, putting on my release and nocking an arrow. I'm sure it took less time and effort getting ready for the high school prom.

Finally settling in, I held my bow down to my side, then watched as my arrow slipped off the string and sped straight to the ground, clanging twice against some brush before landing. I made a mental note to avoid that in the future.

At 9:00 a.m., I repeated the lengthy routine in reverse order and climbed back down the tree. No sign of any deer, ghost buck included.

I decided to give bowhunting another try later in the day on our property just north of town. I dressed as light as anyone could and still be protected from Minnesota's deep woods mosquitoes. Wearing a bug jacket over my camo, I was so warm by the time I reached my stand that I had to remove my steamed glasses for the first hour.

I learned a few good lessons that first evening: It's difficult to draw your bow in a permanent gun stand with walls; a bug jacket will keep out the mosquitoes but is about as breathable as plastic wrap; and the infamous Minnesota mosquito can easily feast on your hands through jersey gloves—most likely with four or five friends. I did get the chance to watch a doe and fawn strolling down the trail. I made another mental note about dropping arrows—this time the arrow actually stuck in to the forest floor.

I had finally cooled off when I descended from my stand and began negotiating my way back through the dark woods. The brush on the trail is thickest by the beaver pond and it's best to move cautiously to avoid falling into "Frank's Hole." This two-foot-wide void in the trail got its name after Frank (a distant relative) involuntarily determined its depth and water temperature a couple of deer seasons ago.

Stubbornly not using my flashlight, I noticed those pretty yellow wildflowers that signal the far edge of the trail (the "watery" far edge of the trail) just as I stepped off solid ground and into water. I can now accurately report that "Frank's Hole" is crotch deep, very cold and quite wet. I sloshed all the way back to the truck, knowing the mosquitoes would attack if I tried to stop and empty my rubber boots.

I decided that my next bowhunt would be after the mosquitoes were tucked in for the winter by mother nature's first frost.

In mid-October, I scouted our woods again and found a sturdy tree with lots of sign and a few rubs in the vicinity. Bordered on the north by a county road, a cow pasture on the east and a cattail slough on the west, this particularly brushy area seems to be a favorite funneling area. The location next to the creek and just 12 yards from the main trail was perfect for my ladder stand.

Settling in for a long wait, I listened intently for a crunch of dry leaves or a snap of a twig. It takes some time to adjust to sitting silently in the woods, but after a while, the stresses at home and pressures at work begin to drift away with the breeze. The crisp autumn air begins to cleanse your lungs, the sounds of birds and squirrels seem to sharpen your hearing and your vision becomes clearer.

A doe and two fawns wandered by the slow-moving creek that evening. A mink did its best to keep me entertained by dancing across the fallen leaves beneath my stand. Two fat gray squirrels played tag as enthusiastically as any kids. One angry little red squirrel barked its disapproval at my presence in its neighborhood. There were mallards using our beaver pond; flocks of them erupted and circled overhead just before dark. I heard the beaver that is trying to turn our woods into wetlands. A grouse looked almost comical as it bounced in the evening breeze sitting on a branch that was slightly too small for its weight.

There emerges a certain fresh, musty, earthy smell in the October woods, and the air was full of it this evening. The skin on my face began to tighten and I could feel the chill through my clothes as the temperature began to drop along with the sun. It was a glorious fall evening to spend in the northwoods.

As I drove home toward a hot supper and a comfortable chair, I realized that this is bowhunting. I know in all the magazine articles that bowhunting is the adrenaline-inducing picture of a big buck in your sights and the sound of the arrow as it races toward its trophy. But I imagine these moments are few, far between and short lived. Most of our hours are spent in solitude, watching nature's grand theater unfold.

I never did arrow a buck my first season, nor did I hunt nearly as often as I had intended. But now that I know what bowhunting is all about, I can't wait until next September. Besides, the ghost buck is still out there.

White-Tailed Deer
Quiz #1
By M.D. Faw
See pages 85 and 86 for the correct answers.

1. Only buck white-tailed deer have antlers.
   a. true
   b. false

2. Hormones from a deer's glands help produce antlers. Which glands?
   a. the testes
   b. the pituitary gland
   c. the thyroid
   d. all of the above

3. The Latin name for the white-tailed deer is *Odocoileus virgini-anus.*
   a. true
   b. false

4. White-tailed deer can weigh up to 300 pounds.
   a. true
   b. false

5. White-tailed deer normally stand four feet tall at the shoulders.
   a. true
   b. false

6. The number of points on a whitetail's antlers indicates age.
   a. true
   b. false

7. The phrase "the buck stops here" is about money.
   a. true
   b. false

8. A white-tailed deer's stomach has four parts.
   a. true
   b. false

9. A popular hunting method for white-tailed deer by early native Americans was stalking while wearing a deer hide and mask.
   a. true
   b. false

10. Which was the first state to enact a law protecting whitetails?
    a. New York
    b. Rhode Island
    c. Pennsylvania

11. A small fawn white-tailed deer has spots to help it blend with
    a. sunlight
    b. flowers

12. A deer has more hairs per square inch in the...
    a. summer
    b. winter

13. A deer sheds hair twice each year.
    a. true
    b. false

14. A deer with a predominantly white coat and brownish spots is called a
    a. piebald
    b. albino
    c. blonde deer

15. A whitetail's tarsal glands are located where?
    a. forehead
    b. neck
    c. inside of rear legs

16. A whitetail's interdigital glands are located where?
    a. near the eyes
    b. between the hooves
    c. on the rump

17. Deer can run at speeds up to 35 mph.
    a. true
    b. false

18. A white-tailed deer's front legs are joined at the shoulders in a ball and socket joint.
    a. true
    b. false

19. Whitetails in the northern regions are bigger than southern whitetails.
    a. true
    b. false

20. Antlers grow from where?
    a. pedicels
    b. glands
    c. holes

21. Antlers are bones.
    a. true
    b. false

The following questions concern distinguishing a mule deer from a white-tailed deer.

22. The major antler beam grows upward on what type of deer?
    a. white-tailed deer
    b. mule deer

23. The antlers grow forks from forks.
    a. white-tailed deer
    b. mule deer

24. Which deer species has the longest metatarsal gland?
    a. white-tailed deer
    b. mule deer

25. Which deer species has a black-tipped tail?
    a. mule deer
    b. white-tailed deer

Our Favorite Kind of Hunter

by NAHC Staff Member
Teri Willenbring

We all hate to sit near him. He's the guy who eats a bag of chips while waiting for his dream buck to appear. He puffs on a cigarette, tobacco filling the crisp morning air. His poor posture in his stand starts to make him uncomfortable, so he shuffles around, rustling the leaves that camouflage his presence.

Alas, he is not camouflaged. And neither are you. The sound, the smell, the sight of him is enough to send even the smallest deer fleeing. Unless you are clear across the field or in another state, your chances of seeing something are slim. True, he may drive deer toward you, but, as we all know, bucks are smart. Sometimes the slightest hint of human presence is enough to keep a field clear of antlers.

Such is the profile of my husband's brother, Stan (not his real name). I learned this the first time I went deer hunting.

When I met Bill, my then-boyfriend and now-husband, he made it clear that any woman of his would not only tolerate his love of hunting but would embrace it as well. I was more than happy to oblige, considering I had been shooting guns since I was 12. Hunting was a logical step.

The family hunting grounds are located in northern Minnesota on 320 acres of private farmland, forest and field owned by Bill's uncle. Generations of Willenbrings have harvested deer on that land. Every year, at least one deer is bagged. Bill intended that my first year would prove to be no exception.

That mid-November hunting day was cold. I was told to dress warmly—very warmly. Fashion was not an option, I mused as I was handed an oversized bright orange jacket and hat. Twenty minutes and seven layers later, I was beginning to sweat. I was determined, however, not to complain about the cold, even if my feet turned to ice cubes.

The only ones hunting that second weekend of the rifle season were Bill, Stan and I. Bill was reluctant to have Stan accompany us to the field. Bill had hunted with Stan in the past and was well aware of his dislike for sitting alone for long periods of time. He knew Stan's apprehension grew greater as darkness fell.

The three of us drove to the field in the forest and dropped Stan off at the northeastern corner. He was to walk a few hundred yards to this stand.

"Now, Stan," Bill said, looking his brother squarely in the eye, "don't be afraid of the dark, and don't, above all, try to find us. We will come and get you when it is time to leave."

He turned to leave. "Understand, Stan?" His brother, six years younger than he, nodded, his jaw firmly set in determination that this year, he would sit still in his stand and finally see a whitetail.

Bill and I drove across the field, parked on the northwest corner and walked along the edge of the woods to our stand. That year, since it was my first time hunting, Bill wanted to sit close by me. We sat on a fallen log, our rifles in hand. There was plenty of brush to keep us camouflaged and just the right amount of space in between to shoot. I sat quieter than I ever had in my life, afraid to move a muscle lest I spook something away and end my hunting career forever. My eyes were fixed on the field before me, watching and waiting for something four-legged and brown.

Suddenly, a deer appeared in front of me just before legal shooting hours were over. It was massive, surely the biggest buck

The author proudly displays the rewards of a successful hunt.

I had ever seen. It was an eight-pointer, weighing around 200 pounds and standing not more than 20 yards from us. Bill carefully raised his semi-automatic .30-06. He leveled the gun, crosshairs directly on his target. He slowly squeezed the trigger and "ping"—a misfire. The buck jerked its head toward us and froze...for a second. A second in which I could have aimed my gun and bagged my first deer. Buck fever took over my senses, however, and the buck hightailed it into the woods.

Bill kept a close eye on it, since the deer hadn't run far. He could see its white tail less than 50 yards away. The possibility was strong that it might venture back to the field if we waited long enough.

But we never got the chance. Instead of hearing the rustle of brush and the snap of twigs as the buck made its way back out, we heard Stan a-callin'.

"Bill! Teri!" he bellowed. "Where are you? Bill!!"

So ended the Willenbring hunting streak—and Stan's hunting career for a few years.

Venison Pasties

2 lbs. venison, ground
1 large onion, chopped
2 cup cooked rutabaga, cubed
1 cup cooked peas
garlic salt
pepper

Pie Crust

3 cups flour
1 cup shortening
1 egg
1½ tsp. vinegar
¾ tsp. salt

Make pie crust (or buy pre-made crust). Cut shortening into flour and salt. Set aside. Put egg in measuring cup and beat. Add vinegar and enough water to make ⅔ cup liquid; mix. Roll dough into six-inch circles on lightly floured board. Lightly brown vension and onion. Stir in rutabaga, peas, garlic salt and pepper. Place ¾ cup of meat mixture in each circle. Fold over and trim edges. Moisten edge with water and press with fork to seal. Pierce top once. Place on cookie sheet and bake at 375 degrees for 20 to 30 minutes. (Makes 12 pastries.)

NAHC Member David Meorsch
Amarillo, TX

Beginner's Luck

*by NAHC Member Larry Duttweiler
of Lawrenceville, Georgia*

*A*lthough I had thought about spending more time in the woods many years earlier, I began deer hunting at age 27. Not long after that, we were blessed with our first child, Billy, and then I shot my first deer on public land in Elbert County, now known as the Heardmont WMA. I began taking Billy with me for some scouting and hunting trips when he was five years old. Of course, he had little or no attention span and those trips were generally a bust for me but a good start for him.

For his seventh birthday, we presented Billy with a bolt action Marlin .22 and as an early eighth birthday present, he received a 20 gauge Winchester youth model pump. Billy was able to take it dove hunting one time before we headed to the October woods for his first actual deer hunting trip.

I had just joined the Trophy Buck Hunting Club in Wilkes County, Georgia, on which 4,000 acres are expertly managed with the use of clear-cuts, mineral blocks, fire breaks and food plots. On opening day I shot a ten-point buck just 20 minutes after sunup. Billy and I went back the next weekend. I got Billy out of school early and he was already wearing his camouflaged pants and beaming with the anticipation of the first big game hunt during which he'd be carrying a loaded firearm. Although he had never seen a deer while hunting with me, he had already been extremely lucky in general. For example, he won Atlanta Braves memorabilia in a raffle, he won a blindfolded basketball shooting contest and he recently won a rod and reel in a raffle from Bass Pro Shop before winning another rod during the Zebco Fish America Series. So I was rather excited about his prospects of at least having a chance to see a deer this weekend.

I had planned on setting up in my friend's stand since he had seen several does during the bow season and even a coyote the week before. Fortunately, he had given me good directions to his stand, which was located about 75 yards inside the woods near a clear-cut feeding area. Billy and I were both able to sit in the stand about 20 feet off the ground and rest our weapons on the padded rail. I told Billy to expect the deer to come most likely from our right side toward the feeding area. Even more important, I reminded my little hunter that the deer in the woods are "gray ghosts" that often appear out of nowhere. Then we settled down to wait on that opportunity.

What I had not told Billy was that I was especially optimistic since there was a storm front about to come through. In fact, it was not long after we settled in at 4:00 p.m. that we could hear thunder in the distance; shortly after that we felt a few raindrops. I grunted softly a few times in order to try to speed up the process in case a buck was traveling nearby in the creekbed ahead of us.

At about this time, Billy told me that we probably ought to head for cover. While I certainly wanted to impress upon my son that I had enough sense to get out of the rain, I tried to persuade him to understand that he might not see such perfect deer hunting conditions again for a long time. About ten minutes after grunting and about 50 minutes after setting up, I noticed some movement out ahead of us and to the left. A good-sized deer ran from our left and headed for an opening ahead of us that was just short of a mineral lick. Since there were only a few scattered pine trees about 30 yards out, I immediately felt that this was going to be a perfect shot opportunity for Billy. Since the deer came up on us so quickly, I reached out to grab the barrel of his shotgun and move it along the rail of the stand ahead of the deer before whispering, "Whenever you're ready..."

To be honest, I froze up watching the scene unfolding before me even though I had promised myself that I would provide back-up with my own .30-06. As the deer came into full view, it slowed to a walk and stepped out 27 yards from the stand .

Just as I was whispering to myself, "NOW!," my little buddy cut loose with a blast from his shotgun, burying a handful of buckshot in the deer's chest. The deer immediately went down, kicked furiously and then got up to run off.

We followed the conventional wisdom—watching where the deer had re-entered the woods—and then attempted to track it both downhill and toward water. We had just about given up when Billy looked to his right side and saw his 145-pound trophy lying on the ground about 75 yards from where he had shot it—apparently after it had circled back and tried to come uphill. I was eager to get closer because in the moment my son had fired his first shot at a deer, it seemed to me that I had seen antlers on what he thought was a doe. We were both right. It was a spike buck with "cowhorn" antlers. One spike was about three inches long and the other was about eight inches long. We guessed that it was about three-and-a-half years old and may have walked under trophy hunters before it was felled by an eight-year-old who could not have been happier with his "trophy buck."

Since then, Billy has shot another button buck and two does with his .30-30 Marlin with a 4X scope. An experienced soccer and baseball player, he still tells everyone who asks that hunting is his favorite sport. While it is wonderful that my "best friend" and I get to go hunting together for years to come, the only problem I have now is that Billy tends to study the advertisements in the back of the magazine for his "dream hunts" for turkey, coyote, wild hogs, elk and pronghorn. His hunting requests led to a trophy boar hunt at the Red Hawk Plantation in Dodge County, Georgia, where we each shot a big hog. In fact, Billy dropped a big boar with a well-placed shot right behind the ear, just as he had been instructed by the lodge's owner. Now Billy wants to move on to his first wild turkey as well as take a deer with his Browning bow, which he tells me he can pull to full draw. I hope the next challenge is always there for him.

I wish some of the northern states would drop their minimum age for hunting, especially big game. Waiting until age 15 is too late for boys who will discover other interests. We will surely lose another generation of hunters if this continues. I cannot predict the future, but the world would probably be a better place if more parents would take their children into the woods to appreciate nature.

Scents And More

- For a low-budget attractor scent, fill a spray bottle with one of the following and spray around your hunting area:

   Apple Juice

   Natural Vanilla Extract

   Mapleine Flavor

   Corn Oil

- When following a blood trail, bring along a spray bottle filled with hydrogen peroxide. If a blood trail is indistinguishable, spray some hydrogen peroxide on the ground. Wherever blood has fallen, the hydrogen peroxide will foam.

- Before taking your dog hunting in snow, trim the hair between the pads of its paws. This will help prevent ice and snow from accumulating between its toes. You might also try fitting your dog with a pair of dog booties used on sled dogs.

Sometimes, common sense gets overlooked. I worked overtime all week just to get caught up enough so I could go hunting on Saturday. Opening day of bow season, I woke up early, and drove 45 minutes to my spot. I was settled in and watching the sky start to brighten. Birds started flying around looking for food, and the squirrels were running through the leaves. The turkeys were sneaking up from behind me, and an owl flew from the tree I was sitting

Stay Ready

by NAHC Member Vincent J. Cox of Akron, Ohio

under. At 8:30 a.m., two does walked up a tree line about 50 yards from me. I watched where they went, and I could see them running around about 100 yards away. After a few minutes, I couldn't see them anymore. I decided to walk up to the point where they had been running around and see what interested them so much in that area. It took me about 20 minutes just to walk 20 yards. I thought I'd better check for legs under the low branches, so I knelt down. Just then the does rounded the corner and headed right for me. They stopped about 15 yards right in front of me and started walking off to my left, heads bobbing and sniffing in my direction. All I could do is watch and enjoy the moment...

See, when I knelt down, I put my crossbow sideways across my body. If I had tried to bring it up, they would have seen me and bolted. If I had it pointed forward, I could have taken a shot faster…

Now I always have the broadhead pointing forward as much as possible!

Gun Safety

Although hunting accidents are down, a single accident is one too many. One of the goals of hunter education programs is to strive toward having zero hunting accidents take place. Some important gun safety rules follow.

- The cardinal rule of gun safety is to treat every gun with the respect due a loaded gun. This means no horseplay with guns.

- One of the most important things you should do when hunting is to be absolutely positive of the identity of your target before you pull the trigger. Remember to keep your gun pointed in a safe direction—don't substitute your scope for binoculars.

- Always carry your gun so that you can control the direction of the muzzle if you stumble. Also, never climb a tree or fence with a loaded gun.

- Make sure you carry only empty guns, taken down or with the action open, into your automobile, camp and home.

- Always be sure that the barrel and action of the gun are clear of obstructions.

- Never leave your loaded gun unattended.

- Do not shoot at flat, hard surfaces or at the surface of water; the bullets may ricochet.

- Never handle a firearm while under the influence of alcohol.

*I*t is the beginning of December, the time every hunter on the face of the earth looks forward to. In my household, Thanksgiving is a time of preparation for the upcoming hunt. As a student, this time off gives my hunting partners and me time to work out strategies and tactics to lure the big one into shooting range. If you are lucky enough to tag a monster buck, you will be praised and honored in my household.

My First Rifle Hunt

by NAHC Member Neil Hallowell of Broomall, Pennsylvania

As the days drag on in November, everyone counts the hours until it's time to leave on the four-hour drive to deer camp. In those hours before we depart, we're like a bunch of bulls in a china shop. Everyone is restless and keeps double-checking his hunting gear. The drive to camp, though, seems to go quickly as we brag about past hunting trips and the deer we have taken. (It seems to be a part of every hunter's program to brag about past trips.)

The night before opening day is pretty quiet as everyone rests for the big day. Then, before I know it, the alarm clock is waking me up at 5:35 a.m. The smell of anxiety is in the air as we dress and head out into the wilderness. My dad usually walks me to my spot and checks to see if everything is all right. Then he walks to his spot and waits patiently. Sitting there in the dark, I question even being out there in the freezing cold at the crack of dawn. But to me, it's worth the scouting and money just to even see a deer.

Suddenly, I hear a loud noise, and two figures appear. Thankfully, it's only deer. It's still quite dark, and the deer pass just five yards away from my stand. I cannot tell if one of them is a buck. Then they catch my scent and take off. Thinking that my chances of getting the big one are over, I sit there until the woods are silent again, and then it hits me—the most awful smell you could imagine. I say to myself that what I am smelling is a buck in rut.

Suddenly, a buck appears about 15 yards away, swaying its massive neck and head up and down in an attempt to locate the two does that had passed by earlier. When the buck is just ten yards away, it turns broadside to me and steps behind two trees. This is my chance! With my gun raised and ready to fire, the buck steps out from behind the trees. I say to myself, it's not the biggest, but it sure will make my dad jealous because of its massive weight. Then it spots me.

I pull the trigger on my lever action rifle. My reaction time is too good and the buck falls to the ground peacefully. Two seconds later my walkie-talkie is full of voices. "Did you get one?" my Dad asks. I answer proudly.

Later, Dad came over and helped me drag it back to camp. Needless to say, getting a deer on the first day of the season is great, but it also has its downfalls—because you now take over as the cook and the housemaid while the others try to fill their tags!

I have always dreamed about hunting for the biggest bucks in the world in Saskatchewan, Canada. Little did I know that my dream would come true. My cousin, Warren, booked a hunt for himself and three other guys. A month later, thankfully, the other three guys backed out. Warren asked my brother, Kyle, our cousin Brandon and me if we would like to fill the three empty spots. Of course we all eagerly jumped at the opportunity.

Saskatchewan Fulfills Member's Dream

by NAHC Member Ryan Stauffeneker of Greer, South Carolina

We soon arrived in Saskatchewan for our exciting six-day hunt. The next day we drove over four hours north to our hunting lodge. There we met our guides Ken Madduck and his son Elliot, who filled our heads full of stories about monster bucks they had seen in the preseason. They said those bucks could be ours!

The following morning we were at our stands before daybreak. The weather was about 15 degrees with light snow, so it was perfect hunting weather. About five minutes after I had settled in my stand, I saw three does, but I was waiting for the monster bucks that Ken had told me about. A few hours later, I saw three more does approaching to the right of my stand. I watched them for a while. They would stop,

NAHC Member Ryan Stauffeneker with a Saskatchewan whitetail.

stomp their feet and look behind them. I thought with great hope that there was a buck behind them, but they walked off and I didn't see anything following them. About 45 minutes later—from the same direction where the does kept looking—came a buck. Standing about 95 yards away from me in thick cover, the buck faced straight at me, so I couldn't quite see its whole rack. When the buck walked a little closer, I couldn't believe my eyes.

I was hunting in a thick patch of woods, but the stand was set on a fenceline going right through the woods. The only place I could shoot was down the fenceline. The buck was closing the distance to the fence, and my heart started racing.

With my 7mm ready, I just waited. The buck jumped the fence and gave me a broadside walking shot. I set my crosshairs just behind his shoulder and squeezed the trigger. He jumped and bucked, so I knew I had made a vital shot. The buck ran about 50 yards before falling. I could not believe my good luck! I had finally gotten the trophy buck I had been dreaming about for so long.

Three hours of hunting in Saskatchewan blessed me with a

21½-inch-spread, 14-point white-tailed buck that scored 172⅜. The Boone and Crockett Club weight of this enormous buck exceeded 400 pounds. I didn't realize just how lucky I was until the last day of our hunt. Warren harvested a decent eight-point. Kyle and Brandon both had opportunities at 150-class deer but came home empty-handed.

I will always be thankful to guides Ken and Elliot for the Saskatchewan hunt of a lifetime

Ryan Stauffeneker (right) and members of his hunting party gather around for this photo and share in the memories of the hunt.

Recycled Inexpensive Trail Markers

Here in Michigan we receive heavy hunting pressure during the deer season. Getting off the beaten path and leaving as little sign as possible is important, but it makes finding your way before and after daylight difficult.

A few years ago I came across an area where the highway department had completed some road construction and found discarded yellow reflective tape workers had used for temporarily marking the the center lines. The tape comes off after a short time and once the road has been painted it is no longer necessary. I found the tape has an adhesive back to it. If you tear the tape in strips about an inch wide and wrap it around tree limbs and brush carefully, it is basically unnoticeable during the day, but coming out of the woods after dark, your flashlight reflects the tape and you "follow the yellow brick road" out. Works the opposite in mornings.

We never mark the trail out to the road. We stop 50 yards or so before coming into the area. Even in the morning you can find your way for 50 yards until you see the tape. Also, if you keep your tape either low and close to the ground or quite high, others will not notice it so easily.

This tape lasts for years, so remove it from state land after the season. We have marked all our trails to tree stands at our private hunting camp. It gives the younger hunters an easy trail to follow to and from their stands.

Mark Outman
Harrison, MI

*I*n 1997, my hunting partner, Monty, and I were drawn for the November whitetail hunt in southern Arizona. We left early Friday morning, the day the hunt started, and decided to do a lot of glassing on the way in to the place where we had decided to camp. By the time we arrived at camp, there were already some other hunters there, so we went to our regular spot on the west side of the mountain range. After setting up a few things, we

My Two Buck Season

by NAHC Member Richard Wetzler
of Tucson, Arizona

hiked around to see if we could spot anything. After three hours of walking and glassing, we went back to camp. We did a little hunting that evening but mostly sat and did a lot of glassing of the surrounding hills. We planned our hunt for the next morning and headed back to camp.

The next morning, we hunted the hills we usually hunt but only saw a couple of does. We hunted back toward camp and talked to a couple of hunters along the road. They had seen a couple of bucks but couldn't get a shot at them.

That evening we hunted the low hills, but all that turned up were a couple does and few tracks. Back at camp that night, we discussed the hunt for the third day. We decided to hunt the hill the same way but to go over the top instead of working the side.

Before daybreak the following morning, we got to the place we had planned to go and started glassing. Within an hour, we spotted seven hunters in front of us. We let them make their move, then headed toward the top of the mountain. We jumped a doe out in

NAHC Member Richard Wetzler with the buck he bagged in Arizona.

front of us and kept walking. We spotted two hunters who had seen the doe and had their glasses on her. After waiting a few minutes to see what they were going to do, we headed on up the ridge. When we got close to the end of the ridge, I dropped off the side and began to work my way around the point to meet Monty on the other side. Monty walked through a small saddle and went off the edge. The terrain was steep and rocky with a lot of thick bush; I tried my best to be quiet, but that didn't work. As I was rounding the point, a whitetail buck jumped in front of me; all I could see were antlers and a big white tail. I figured he would run into Monty. I hurried to get around the mountain but couldn't, so I looked down the hill below me. The buck must have seen Monty and gone downhill because I saw it, put my crosshairs behind its shoulders and squeezed the trigger. The buck jumped straight up and took off running. I watched it run a short distance and top over a ridge. When it disappeared, I made note of a yucca break for a reference point.

When I met up with Monty, I explained what had happened. Since I hadn't see the buck run out of the canyon, I thought it was probably still in there. When we came to the broken yucca, I told Monty that the buck should be in this area. Then I turned around and there it was: a perfect 3x3 Coues' deer. The next day at the taxidermists, the deer scored 102 points.

So with my firearms deer hunt over, I had to concentrate on the archery deer and javelina season. When the archery season opened, I started hunting as soon as I could in an area south of Tucson where I've hunted before. On my fourth day of hunting, I called in a doe early in the morning but decided to keep hunting. At about 10:00 a.m., I started heading back toward the truck. When I came over this little ridge and was approaching some mesquites in the bottom of a small draw, a mule deer buck came out with his nose to the ground. Since there wasn't any cover between us, I went down on my knees. I figured he would run as soon as the nock snapped on the string; I muffled the sound with my fingers. The buck walked behind the only tree between us and I drew. He stopped and looked dead at me for at least two minutes. I had already put my sight pin on him when he decided that the coast was clear and started walking. I touched the trigger on my release, heard my arrow go through the mesquites and watched the buck run off. I watched him for about 150 yards, then he disappeared.

When I walked down to find my arrow and look for any sign of a hit, I saw an arrow lying under a tree, but it was the wrong color of shaft and fletching. The closer I got to it, the more it looked like mine. Then it dawned on me: It was mine covered in blood.

I had planned to wait half an hour before tracking the deer, but adrenalin took over. I started looking for sign and flagging the area where the buck had run off. I came to a creek bottom in the area where I last had seen the buck running and glassed there for a few minutes but saw no sign of it. When I walked over to the top of the ridge at my left, I saw something in the bottom of the draw that looked like a cholla cactus skeleton. I put my glasses on the object; it was the buck's left horn sticking up. I got excited and started to work my way down to it when I remembered to nock an arrow just in case the buck tried to get up. When I got closer, I could see that its eyes were open and that it was dead. He was a beautiful 5x4 mule deer buck.

I called the taxidermist the next morning, and he gave me a rough green score of about 176 points gross. I told him that my whitetail buck would have to wait, that this mule deer was the one to mount!

What a great way to end a year and a great way to begin one.

It Can Warm You Up

Here's a tip that will warm you when you are cold and keep you warm for many hours. What you need can probably be found in the house right now: an empty 13-ounce coffee can, a roll of toilet paper and a bottle of isopropyl alcohol, otherwise known as rubbing alcohol. In order to fit, some of the toilet paper usually needs to be taken off. Be sure it fits snugly and roll up the excess toilet paper to fill the hole between the cardboard roll. Pour the alcohol in until the roll of toilet paper is nicely saturated and reseal the can with the plastic cap. Remove cap and light the paper/alcohol when you're on your deer stand or otherwise out in the cold, and you'll have a nice, steady source of heat. This is also great to keep behind the seat of the truck in case of emergency.

Gabriel Kalmar
Westminister, CO

White-Tailed Deer
Quiz #2
See pages 86 and 87 for the correct answers.

1. How long do a deer's antlers have to dry before they can be officially scored for the record books?
   a. 30 days
   b. 60 days
   c. 90 days
   d. 2 weeks

2. Which state sells the most hunting licenses?
   a. Minnesota
   b. Montana
   c. Pennsylvania
   d. California

3. A white-tailed deer is an ungulate. What does this mean?
   a. It has a four-part stomach.
   b. It can sleep standing up.
   c. It runs faster than 35 mph.

4. Antler development of a white-tailed buck peaks at what age?
   a. 5 years
   b. 10 years
   c. 2 years

5. A deer needs what minerals to grow antlers?
   a. protein
   b. phosphorus
   c. calcium
   d. all of the above

6. White-tailed deer became America's most popular hunting
   species in which decade?
   a. 1960s
   b. 1970s
   c. 1980s

7. What state has one of the most liberal white-tailed deer hunting seasons? Hint: The season lasts more than three months and allows "a buck a day."
    a. Alabama
    b. Florida
    c. Pennsylvania

8. What state has one of the earliest opening days for whitetail season? Hint: It's in August!
    a. South Carolina
    b. Mississippi
    c. Virginia

9. The estimated number of deer hunters in the United States is:
    a. 10 million
    b. 50 million
    c. 65 million

10. Antler rattling for white-tailed bucks is credited with originating in which state?
    a. Texas
    b. Alabama
    c. Missouri

M y mind flashed back to the day he was born. His first hunting outfit was a camouflage suit made for a doll. Now he stood over his first buck, a beautiful nine-point whitetail.

I have hunted all of my life and over the years have enjoyed my share of success. Of all the trophies I've taken, none were more exciting to me than the nine-point buck that my son, Andrew, took during his first year of deer hunting.

Passing the Tradition

by NAHC Member Kevin Howard of Elsberry, Missouri

I have to admit I had been hoping for a boy when Andrew was born. Elaine and I already had a beautiful three-year-old daughter. A healthy baby—boy or girl—would have been great, but a son to share the outdoors with and play sports with and be my best buddy was what I was hoping for.

That's not to say a daughter can't share all of those things with her dad. My daughter, Erin, who likes to shoot, went hunting with me when she was small and is great at cleaning fish. But there is a bond between a father and son or mother and daughter that is special.

By the time Andrew was three, he was tagging along with me on fishing and hunting trips. He enjoyed getting dressed up in hunting clothes and carrying his toy guns with me to the woods. A friend of mine made me a blind that looks like a big round bale of hay, and it was a perfect way to take a small child hunting. Andrew could take small toys to play with and food and drink to keep him happy. Over the years, he saw all kinds of wildlife from the blind, and I could take the time to talk to him about hunting.

I started teaching both of my kids to shoot by the time they were five or six. Their first guns were Daisy Red Rider BB guns. I taught them how to handle a gun safely both at the bench and in the field. We made the shooting sessions fun by shooting a variety of targets including paper and action targets made by the air gun companies.

The kids quickly advanced to .22 rifles from the air guns. Something about the "bang" made them more interested in the rimfire guns. Because my guns were too big for the kids to handle safely, I purchased one of the small .22 single-shot bolt guns made by Oregon Arms called the "Chipmunk." Everything about the gun is made for the small frame of a young person. Andrew could shoulder and shoot the Chipmunk just like I do my rifles. We even put a scope on it in later years to start preparing Andrew for hunting.

When Andrew was about three, I got a good deal on a youth model Winchester 1300 20 gauge shotgun. I knew when I bought it that it would be several years before he would use it, but it has been a great first shotgun. The gun is scaled for a smaller person with a shorter and smaller stock. From the factory it only holds one shell. However, as the shooter becomes more proficient, the plug in the magazine can be shortened so the gun can hold two or three shells.

From the time he was three, Andrew has spent countless hours in the woods with me looking for deer or turkey sign and helping me get stands ready for hunting season. I have shown him deer trails and buck sign like rubs and scrapes. We have scouted turkeys before the season, getting up early to hear the gobblers before fly-down time. The more he has seen and experienced, the more he has wanted to participate.

In Missouri where I live, a youth must be 11 years old and have passed a hunter safety course before he or she can hunt deer or turkeys. They can, however, under the supervision of an adult, hunt small game and birds before that. I decided that for Andrew's first hunting experience we would go after squirrels on our farm. Our squirrel season runs from the last Saturday in May until January 15 of the next year. Andrew was ten the first year he went hunting.

It was early January and squirrels were still gathering acorns from the leaf-covered forest floor. That afternoon, Andrew carried his 20 gauge shotgun and I had a .22 rifle. The first couple of squirrels we saw were too far for his shotgun, so I took them with my .22. When the sun started to set, we began working our way back to the truck. It looked like Andrew was going to have to wait for another day to take his first squirrel.

I was leading the way up a game trail on the last hill before we reached the truck when a squirrel scurried up a small tree about 25 yards in front of me. Andrew moved in front of me but had a hard time finding the squirrel that was holding tightly to the trunk. I knelt down and let him use my six-power binocular to scan the top of the tree. With the aid of the binocular, he quickly found the squirrel's hiding place.

Taking careful aim, he squeezed the trigger like we had practiced at the range. The squirrel tumbled out of the tree as soon as the gun went off. We both whooped and hollered and ran to retrieve Andrew's first game animal. Andrew said his heart was beating fast from the excitement of looking for the squirrel and then making the shot. I told him I hoped that feeling would never stop as long as he hunted. He immediately asked me if we could have the squirrel mounted for his room. I told him we might wait for something bigger, like a deer.

Andrew's 11th birthday fell after our spring turkey season, so he couldn't hunt turkeys that year. However, he did look forward to fall when he could join the ranks of deer hunters and participate in our annual family deer hunt.

Like most states, Missouri requires everyone born after a certain date to take a hunter education course. In Missouri, it is anyone born after 1967. At some point in the future, everyone who hunts in Missouri will have to have taken this course. I had been through the course a couple of times but took the opportunity to take it again with Andrew. It was a good time for me to go over the safety aspects of hunting and share the experience with my son. I know we are closer because I took the time to be with him as he learned more about hunter safety and conservation. Even though I had been teaching him about these subjects since he was small, we both learned many things from the course.

The hunter education course ran for several hours Friday night and all day Saturday. Andrew passed the test with flying colors, and we immediately went to buy his deer license. I wanted to give him something special to commemorate his passing the

Deer season was next on the hunting agenda...

course, so we looked at hunting knives at the sporting goods store. We ended up settling on a Buck knife and sheath. It is and will always be a special knife for him.

Andrew's second hunting experience came on September 1 that year: the annual opening day of dove season. We had practiced with his 20 gauge shotgun, first shooting stationary targets, then moving up to clay birds thrown off a portable thrower. Eye-hand coordination and good reflexes must be part of being young. With some coaching, Andrew quickly became very proficient at hitting clay targets.

The practice really paid off when a dove floated across the wheat field we were hunting—Andrew took it with his first shot. What made it even more special was Angel, Andrew's two-year-old yellow Lab, who proudly retrieved the dove for him. With several doves working the field, Andrew was able to take numerous shots. He quickly became addicted to the fast-paced shooting.

Deer season was next on the hunting agenda, and a lot of thought, time and effort went into the preparation. We have an excellent deer herd on our farm, and I was confident Andrew would get a shot. I wanted to be sure he was ready when the time came.

Andrew's deer rifle was to be a Ruger Model 77 in the 6.5 x 55 Swedish caliber. This is an excellent deer cartridge for a young shooter. The 140-grain Winchester Super X Power Point bullets we use in it work great on deer while keeping the recoil manageable for a smaller person. The shooting and practice sessions started with the scope-mounted .22 rifle. The sight picture in the one-inch scope is the same as the scope on the deer rifle. The inexpensive .22 ammunition allows for a lot of shooting practice.

From the .22 we moved up to a .22 Magnum, which let us increase the shooting distance. A .22 Magnum can shoot very good groups out to 100-150 yards. This gun let Andrew practice at distances he would likely be shooting at deer.

Andrew's first experience with a center-fire rifle was a .22-250 Winchester model 70 Featherweight. This gun has basically the same feel as a deer rifle. The gun can be shot at any reasonable distance that someone would shoot at a deer. The .22-250 cartridge has very little recoil and is easily managed by an 11-year-old. It was a lot of fun for Andrew to be hitting targets at 150 yards with the gun.

To make it a little more exciting, we took all the leftover watermelons and pumpkins from our garden and set them up at various ranges. I would pick out a target and Andrew would see how fast he could get in position to shoot the watermelon or pumpkin.

When Andrew had become proficient with the .22-250, we moved up to the Ruger he would hunt with. Again, we shot at various ranges and then started shooting at a life-sized paper deer target. This really gave him a good idea of the area he needed to aim at on the deer.

A few weeks before deer season, we started scouting for the best place to set up our treestand. We ended up setting the stand on the side of a hill above a creek in a hardwood section of woods. Several deer trails crisscrossed within 150 yards of the stand. In final preparation, we set up targets at various ranges and directions from the stand. Andrew practiced shooting at these targets from the stand during the middle of the day a couple of weeks before the season.

On opening morning, Andrew and I settled into our stand just before daylight. We pulled our guns up and waited for first light. It was barely light enough to see when I heard a deer walking toward us from in front of the stand. I could see the six-point buck in my binocular, but neither Andrew nor I could see it with the naked eye. The deer passed within 40 yards but never gave Andrew a chance for a shot.

Andrew had two deer tags; one for a doe or anterless deer and one for a buck or a doe. He had told me the night before that he planned to try and take the first deer he could. At about 7:00 a.m., a doe, fawn and small five-point buck started down a trail to our left. If they stayed on course, they would come within a few yards of the tree to which we had the stand attached.

Andrew got his gun ready and looked at the deer through his scope. He picked his head up off the stock and told me the buck was too small and he was going to take the doe. I don't think we should make trophy hunters out of new hunters, but I was proud of Andrew for wanting to shoot a bigger buck. His patience would pay off later.

As the deer turned and stopped at about 50 yards, Andrew took careful aim at the doe and shot. After I saw the bullet strike perfectly just behind the shoulder, the doe ran about 30 yards and fell. Because Andrew was in front and below me a little, he didn't see it fall. We unloaded our guns, let them down and climbed out of the stand. After reloading, we began following the blood trail, and I let him find the doe. He was ecstatic with his first deer. We hugged, took pictures and gave thanks for our good fortune before field dressing the deer. After getting the deer checked in at the local check station, we hung it in a shed, had lunch and headed back to the woods. We both spent the rest of the afternoon playing the events of the morning hunt over and over again in our minds.

The next morning we were back in our stand looking for a bigger buck. At about 7:30 a.m., I saw a deer sneaking through the woods from the general direction from which the deer the day

Proud NAHC Member Kevin Howard (left) followed a series of steps to prepare his son, Andrew, for the moment of sucess with his first deer.

before had come. I could tell it was a buck through my binocular and when it stopped in an opening at about 100 yards, I could see it was a nice ten-pointer. I tried to help Andrew see the deer, but because he was a little lower and in front of me in the stand, he could not see it. After a minute or two, the buck walked off in the direction of my brother's stand. When we heard him shoot, we figured he had the buck. It turned out we were right, and Andrew's uncle had a 130-class Boone and Crockett Club buck.

Although Andrew was disappointed he had not been able to see the deer, he was happy for his uncle and determined to get a buck of his own. After helping get the buck out, Andrew was ready to get back to hunting. Because we knew it could be a long afternoon, we decided to hunt from my brother's tower-stand, a box blind set on 12-foot legs. It is comfortable and easily holds two people.

We had taken snacks and drinks with us so we could last out the afternoon. We even took turns taking naps. At about 3:00 p.m. things began to happen. First, a doe came out to feed, then two does and two fawns followed. By 4:30 p.m., we had seen a dozen does and fawns.

Andrew Howard with his first white-tailed buck.

As another doe entered the field, she kept looking back, so I suspected a buck was following her. I glanced back into the woods and saw a nice buck coming up the trail the last doe had just used.

All through the afternoon Andrew had practiced getting his gun up on the does and fawns. To get a good angle and rest, he had to sit on my knees. Again, practice paid off, and he was quickly and quietly ready when the buck stepped out of the woods. He let the buck walk about 40 yards out in the field and took the shot when the buck stopped. The deer jumped and headed back down the trail. I was confident Andrew had made a good shot, and with fading light we quickly followed to look for the deer.

I was the first one to see the downed deer and let out a whoop. Andrew ran over to see his buck, a beautiful nine-pointer. My brother, dad and a close friend who hunts with us showed up a few minutes later to see Andrew's deer. It was a special moment as I spread some of the buck's blood on Andrew's face: a tradition hunters who have killed their first buck on our farm go through. The pictures of a smiling 11-year-old with his buck tell the story.

I couldn't have been more proud of Andrew. He worked hard and prepared for the deer season. He practiced his shooting and knew he could hit what he was shooting at. I was also proud of him for passing on a smaller buck the day before because it wasn't what he wanted. And, yes, we did have the buck mounted and it is proudly displayed in Andrew's bedroom.

There is a special bond between Andrew and me because of the time we have spent together getting ready for hunting and then hunting together. Besides being my son, he is one of my best friends. Through hunting, he has learned respect for firearms and the responsibility it takes to be a good hunter.

As the late famous trick shooter for Winchester, Herb Parsons, would say at the close of his program, "Take your son hunting and you won't have to hunt for him." I don't think I'll have to worry about hunting for Andrew.

Reasons Hunters Hunt

Hunters hunt for recreation and to be with friends. However, certain game species also lure hunters afield. The following species are hunters' favorite reasons for heading afield:

deer	91%
squirrels and rabbit	45%
turkeys	40%
pheasant, doves and quail	35%

Shape Up For Better Hunting

When gun deer season opens, some hunters will have a miserable experience. The weather may be ideal. Mornings may be crisp and cool, with warmer temperatures calling for shedding a garment or two in midday. A hunter may bag a fine eight-point buck, but before the day is over, this same hunter will be in misery.

Why the gloomy scenario? The hunter's poor physical condition is the basic reason. And it can be avoided fairly easily, according to Marc Kilburn of the Arkansas Game and Fish Commission.

Yes, physical conditioning should be a year-round concern for a hunter. Short of that, the hunter should begin getting himself in shape several months before hunting. But just a few weeks from gun deer season, the hunter may think back to the past and recall huffing and puffing after a short walk up a small hill or through heavy brush.

He or she may also recall downing a deer and struggling to get it out of the woods. The physical task can even be life-threatening. Heart attacks from overexertion by wrestling with a deer carcass have claimed lives.

Two basic plans are voiced by veteran hunters: 1) If you are already an active person, step up the pace a little in preparation for deer hunting. 2) If you are badly out of shape—a couch potato—do what you can for physical preparation, then realize your limitations when you're in the field.

For starters, take a brisk walk each day you possibly can. Walk, don't jog. Start off with a walk of 20 to 30 minutes, but don't go past the point of pleasant tiredness. If you feel exhausted, you've done too much. If it's raining, use a stationary bicycle.

A 20-minute walk should take you about a mile. If you take much more time to cover a mile, you're probably walking too slowly for efficient exercise. Increase the distance a little every few days. Again, use your judgment and keep to the yardstick of a pleasant tiredness at the end of the walk. Another yardstick is to be able to converse with a companion during the walk; if you gasp for breath trying to talk after walking 15 or 20 minutes, you're probably overdoing it.

If you plan to hunt in hilly or mountainous terrain, climb some stairs in addition to or during your walk. One method is to use a high school or college football field; most are open to community walkers. Walk a lap or two, then climb the steps to the top of the stadium and return for another lap or two of walking. The effects will be beneficial, even over just a short period.

For general exercise walking, a good pair of shoes is not only desirable, it's a necessity. Manufacturers have realized the need for shoes for exercise walking, and you'll find them at most stores.

It's a good idea to shift to your hunting boots or whatever footwear you'll use when deer season opens for the last two or three exercise walks before the season. Your feet need to become accustomed to these boots that may not have been in use since last deer season. Since boots are heavier than shoes, legs will tire more rapidly when wearing them.

Source: Arkansas Game & Fish Commission

"This is the place. I feel it!" I whispered to David Blanton, Realtree Outdoors' ace cameraman and a longtime friend and hunting partner. "If my hunch is right, it'll come right through there." I spoke softly, pointing in the direction of a trail almost directly in front of us.

Quickly, David set up the camera and pointed it in the general direction of the trail. When he was all set with the camera's adjustments, David gave me the thumbs-

Mental Games of Hunting

by Larry Weishuhn,
North American Hunter
"Whitetails" Columnist

up sign. I started rubbing a nearby limb with my rattling horns. I had scarcely started horning the limb when a decent eight-point white-tailed buck came running toward us, exactly down the trail I had expected it to. The buck milled around momentarily before staring back in the direction it had come. Then out stepped a much bigger, fully mature eight-point, this one with about a 20-inch spread with extremely long tines and good mass. This was a good buck but still not the one we were looking for that morning.

During the next 15 minutes, we rattled up a total of eight bucks of varying size—at least a couple of which I would have gladly taken had I been hunting anywhere else—but I knew there was one particularly big white-tailed buck in the area. Or at least I felt there should be. No one had seen such a buck there; I just had a feeling there was a monster in the area.

After the last buck appeared, we waited another 15 minutes to see if there were any more bucks coming in to the rattling horns. When nothing else showed, we stood up and started walking back to the pickup to find another place to follow other hunting hunches.

"Why'd you choose the exact spot we rattled?" queried David. "It really didn't look that much different from any other place on the property."

"I just had a feeling—a hunch—that spot would be productive," I offered. "I can't really explain it." I don't really think it is anything mystical. I think the best explanation for hunting hunches is that you subconsciously pick up on things, things such as there's good cover and food in the area or maybe you even smell bucks without realizing it. I don't know how to explain it, but I have always found that if I play hunting hunches they generally pay off, whether I'm rattling or setting up a treestand. I also think everyone who hunts has such "hunches," yet far too often they are too busy hunting to pick up on them. Maybe they're trying too hard to be successful that they're not listening or paying attention to feelings one gets about a particular area.

Starting to sound pretty far out? Perhaps, but I really don't think so. Hunting in many respects is a mental game, beyond trying to match wits with an animal who lives in the area we only visit a few days a year. I think we have to be mentally prepared for what is going to happen when we go to the field.

If you are thinking about work, squabbles with family or friends, where else you should be hunting or any multitude of other mental distractions, you will not be paying full attention to your surroundings. By thinking about things other than hunting and your surroundings and not paying attention, you'll very possibly miss the twitch of an ear or the wiggle of a tail.

When I was a youngster, my dad used to tell me when he left me in a deer stand, usually a treestand, to "stay awake." He was not concerned I was going to go to sleep but that I pay attention to

*The author won his mental
game with this nice buck in
the Texas brush country.*

everything going on around me, with my senses of sight, hearing and smell working at full capacity.

If you are mentally alert, you will pick up more quickly on movement in the brush; you'll be able to react more quickly when a deer appears and you'll make a humane and killing shot.

A lot of times when I'm in the deer woods, especially with the hectic schedule I keep and the distances I travel, I get mentally and physically tired. I used to fight it. As I have gotten older I have learned that the best thing for me to do, especially if I'm so tired I am not at peak attentiveness, is to simply crawl out of my stand, find a safe place on the ground and take a brief nap. I might as well get some rest and wake up refreshed because if I'm dozing mentally anyway, I'm going to miss what is going on around me. It is better to take a nap and be ready and "awake" to all my surroundings. The next time you get really tired, relax for a little while, but don't do it sitting in your treestand!

Another mental aspect of hunting white-tailed bucks—especially big, mature bucks—is to realize that such bucks are completely different from younger bucks. When hunting mature bucks, you need to be mentally prepared for failure, in that you may not take a buck some years. Not all of us who hunt are going to take game every year as it is, and there can be many reasons why we don't that are totally out of our control. Fortunately, many times there are factors we can control. Such factors include deciding where to hunt and our mental attitude while hunting.

Several years ago, a very dear friend of mine started hunting whitetails after many years of hunting mule deer, elk and various other game. He wanted a sizable white-tailed buck so badly that he could scarcely contain himself. Unfortunately, mental errors cost him several opportunities. I used to accuse him of "outthinking himself." I would set him up in a stand and return later to find him gone and set up in a completely different area. Yet, right where I had left him were fresh tracks over the top of my morning's boot prints, and green shavings where a buck had rubbed its antlers at the base of rubs nearly under my friend's stand.

When he would see a decent-sized buck, he would go bonkers and forget all he knew about hunting and shooting—like taking a solid rest before squeezing the trigger. He would shoot far too quickly and rush his shot.

Big whitetails never give you much time to see, evaluate, estimate the distance and execute the shot. Seldom if ever will they give you more than five seconds. I agree that is not a long time, but if you rush your shot, you'll blow it.

My friend was simply wound too tightly mentally. While I think hunting is definitely a mental game, he had gone a couple of turns of the crank too far. It took about three years of hard hunting for him to loosen up just a bit. When he finally did, he started taking good bucks!

I am an advocate of using scents and lures. In some instances, they work from a biological aspect, and that is important! But the biggest reason they "work" is from a mental aspect. If you use scents and lures and believe they are going to help you take a deer, they will! My reasoning is that if you use such hunting aids and believe in them, you are going to be paying attention because you expect something to happen at any moment. Then when it does, you will pick up on it immediately.

Learn to listen to what your mind is trying to tell you and follow up on hunting hunches. Your mental hunting attitude may well mean the success or failure of a hunting trip.

I had been hunting all my spare time during October and had seen a nice eight-point two times but could not get a clean shot at him. I saw a lot of does but no horns after that period. I was at home one day when my brother-in-law called to let me know that a big buck had just come into his farm's back field with a six-point. The deer were fighting when he came to call me.

Stalking the Fighter

by NAHC Member John Satterwhite of Flashing, Michigan

When I got to his house, the six-point with a broken antler was leaving. Looking through binoculars, we spotted the other buck bedded. All we could see was about three inches of horns above the weeds. We planned a stalk. After about 20 minutes of crawling through the muddy field, I found myself 19 yards from this big buck. Suddenly, the wind changed. Pinned down with no place to go, I motioned for my brother-in-law to walk the nearby fencerow.

Somehow everything clicked, and the big buck started to watch my brother-in-law as he walked the fencerow. When the buck finally had its head turned all the way across its rump, I stepped four yards into the weed field and was lined up straight on for a shot with my bow. The big buck lay bedded

John Satterwhite with his 10-point whitetail. He successfully stalked and arrowed the buck while it was bedded in an open weed field.

looking over his rump and never saw me.

I drew my bow, placed the sight pin on the deer's rack and followed its neck down to its chest. My arrow found its mark with a perfect neck pass-through shot. The buck sprang to its feet and dashed off only to collapse 50 yards away.

I believe the big buck let its guard down a little after a hard-fought battle with the six-point. I made a successful stalk that will be remembered every time I look at this fine buck—a ten-pointer with an 18-inch spread—hanging on my wall.

A Hunter's Dream

To be a carpenter,
You need a hammer and a beam;
To be a hunter,
You need to have a dream,
A dream to get a buck,
Or to shoot that wild duck.
Maybe you go to get the best,
Or maybe you want to get some rest.
Maybe you want to go
To try out your bow,
But only see a doe.
Maybe next time you'll have better luck;
Maybe you'll see a monster buck.
A dream is the reason
You'll come back next season.

Philip Voisin
of Menomonee Falls,
Wisconsin

Photo courtesy of Rick O'Shea

Treestand Tips

Step Holes Are Easy to Find

Many hunters remove the bottom three or four screw-in tree steps to keep other hunters out of their treestand or to deter thieves. Inserting a small twig in the hole may help to relocate screw holes the following morning. Placing a reflective thumbtack around the hole is another option.

A Useful Spare Step

If you use steps to climb to your treestand, always put an extra step at the same height as the stand's seat and around to the side of the stand. You can use this spare step to assist you as you climb onto the stand. After you are on the stand, the extra step is a great place to hold a day pack, canteen or other gear.

Build a Better Stand

You can make your treestand less noticeable by securing brushy limbs along its bottom to help break up the stand's outline. With pruning shears and wire, this project takes only a few minutes. Be sure that no limbs are near your feet or you may spook game if you have to move slightly before taking a shot.

Don't Fight the Dark

If your treestand requires adjustable bolts that have knobs or wingnuts, covering them with reflective tape can make them easier to find if they fall to the ground. Many stores have the inexpensive reflective tape in their automotive section. Also put a strip of tape on the bottom of your stand.

Wear That Safety Belt

Many treestand accidents occur as the hunter is entering or exiting the stand. Besides placing an extra tree step near the stand to hold onto, you should always wear your safety belt when climbing onto or off of the stand. Always wear a safety belt while you are in a treestand.

Here are ten quick tips to help you bag your next deer:

1 Go hunt! All too often, it is easier to sit at home or in camp lamenting about the cold weather, hot weather, rain, fog or even the moon phase. Only under extremely rare circumstances can you be a successful deer hunter sitting in camp!

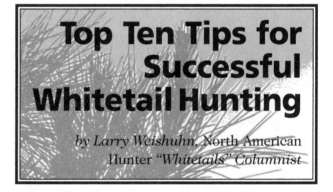

Top Ten Tips for Successful Whitetail Hunting

by Larry Weishuhn, North American Hunter "Whitetails" Columnist

2 Become intimately knowledgeable of your bow's or gun's capabilities as well as your own capabilities. If you shoot a gun, learn how to shoot both left- and right-handed. Shoot from a solid rest, whether the shot is near or far. The biggest complaint I get from whitetail guides and outfitters is that hunters are poor shots, simply because they have not spent enough time shooting—especially from "real-life hunting situations."

3 Adopt the "five seconds to success" rule, which simply states that a big, mature buck is seldom (if ever) going to give you more than five seconds to see him, evaluate his age and antlers, estimate the distance and make a killing shot.

4 Rather than scouting right before the opening of hunting season, do your scouting immediately after the season closes. Make notes about where you find rubs, scrapes and other deer sign such as shed antlers. Maintain a map of your hunting areas that includes sightings of rubs, scrapes and shed antlers. Too much preseason scouting immediately before the season will cause mature bucks to alter their routines, leave the immediate area or possibly become totally nocturnal.

5 Search for places within your hunting area where other hunters do not hunt—possibly an extremely dense thicket, near a house or home or even camp, or in a tall and open grass field. Bucks, especially mature bucks that have survived several deer seasons, adapt to the ways of us mere humans. They pattern us a whole lot more successfully than we could ever hope to pattern them. They go to bed and hide in places that hunters do not frequent.

6 If you locate a dense thicket with much deer sign during post-season scouting, return to it during the winter and cut some narrow shooting lanes in the center of the thicket, stopping before you reach the edge of the thicket. The following fall, hunt that thicket, but get into it long before daylight, before the buck enters its bedding area. It's a long, silent vigil, but the rewards could well be worth the efforts!

7 Be confident you are going to take a deer every time you go to the woods. Have a positive attitude. One of the reasons scents and lures work as well as they do is because the hunters who use them pay attention to what is going on around them and expect things to happen. When it does, they'll seize the moment!

8 Patience is not only a virtue, it is often the key to taking a deer. Patient hunters move very little, and when they do, they do so very slowly, rather than in jerky movements. A patient hunter also stays in the woods much longer and generally hunts all day long. Often, the big, mature bucks move only

during the middle of the day. Patience also means passing up shots at young bucks in hopes of taking an old mossback.

9 Successful hunters are open to new techniques or dare to try something different, such as using scents, lures, rattling antlers or decoys, as well as hunting different areas.

10 Be persistent. Continue hunting until the last moment of the last legal day. Quite often big bucks are taken at the last moment of the hunt. (But also be prepared to go home empty handed if you set your goal as a big buck or nothing.)

Employ the top ten tips for successful whitetail hunting, and you too can bring home bucks like this. Here's Larry Weishuhn with a nice buck.

A Look At Outdoor Economics

Whether a young hunter using paper route savings to buy a first shotgun, a business executive writing a $4,000 check for the elk hunt of a lifetime or an angler paying $4.50 for an early morning breakfast, America's outdoor heritage fuels our economy at a pace rivaled by few sports and few industries.

Hunters and anglers contribute nearly $40 billion to the U.S. economy each year. The average sportsman contributes $1,024, totaling $7 billion for food and lodging, $5 billion in real estate leases, $900 million in permits, licenses, stamps and other regulated fees, and $19 billion for equipment.

Each year, more than one million jobs are directly or indirectly supported by hunting and fishing. Each day, hunting produces enough economic activity to support one thousand jobs. For every 50 hunters, enough economic activity is generated to create one job.

Of course, dollars and cents alone do not represent the true worth of our outdoor traditions. Wealthier than any millionaire is one with greater awareness of and respect for the natural environment and its wildlife. Wealthier still is one who can share this treasure with a youngster, friend or relative.

Here's What Hunters Are Doing For Our Wildlife:

Then		Now
500,000	In 1900, an official U.S. survey estimated that fewer than 500,000 white-tailed deer remained in the nation. Today, some 18 million whitetails roam our forests.	18,000,000
1,110,000	Habitat destruction reduced Canada goose populations to around 1,110,000 in the late 1940s. Since then, the population has more than tripled.	3,760,000
41,000	In 1907, only about 41,000 elk were counted in the U.S. Today, there are about 800,000, and most western states have surplus populations.	800,000
100,000	By the early 1900s, encroaching civilization and habitat loss had reduced wild turkey populations to 100,000. Conservation programs have now restored the turkey to healthy numbers in 41 states.	4,500,000
12,000	About 50 years ago, the total U.S. population of pronghorn antelope was about 12,000. Habitat restoration and restocking have helped to restore it to more than 1 million.	1,000,000

Source: National Shooting Sports Foundation

The fall deer hunting season had been over about a month or so before I could make my way back to one of my favorite hunting places. Normally, I try to return to do my post-season scouting no later than two weeks after the season closes. By then the deer are back to a "normal" routine and really do not pay a lot of attention to someone walking through the woods.

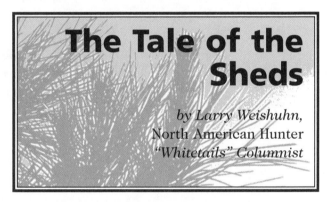

The Tale of the Sheds

by Larry Weishuhn,
North American Hunter
"Whitetails" Columnist

For years I have maintained a journal about what I find on scouting trips, especially where I locate rubs and scrapes after the hunting season is over. I learned a long time ago that bucks frequently return year after year to the same scrapes. They also rub on the same trees—or at least in the same general area—time and again, as evidenced by old scarring on the trees and saplings. Where I find these rubs and scrapes is the area I'll hunt the following fall.

One of the other important buck signs I look for during my post-season scouting trips is cast or shed antlers, especially those from sizable bucks. On a map of my hunting area, I make particular note of any sheds I find and exactly where I have found them. My shed antler maps are topo maps, aerial photo maps and even hand-drawn maps to be even more specific about exactly where I've found a shed antler.

Why all the interest in sheds, or cast pieces of bone? Quite frequently, they are the key that unlocks the "where does he live" mystery. Sheds also verify the size of a buck and indicate the buck made it through the hunting season. Perhaps more important, they tell me exactly where that buck was at a particular point in time when its antlers dropped.

Larry Weishuhn records deer activity.

Over the years I have taken several good mature bucks within less than 200 yards of where I found his sheds the previous winter! It has happened far too many times to be a coincidence. Several years ago I picked up two big shed antlers on one of the properties I hunted at the time. I found them about a hundred yards apart. Both sides had main beams of 28 inches and a total of five points per side. The shortest tines were its browtines, about 6 inches. Its longest tines were 14 inches. It had fair mass as well. Giving it an inside spread of approximately 17 inches the buck would have easily net scored 170 Boone and Crockett Club points.

In comparing the diameter of its main beam just above the burr to the pedicel area (where the antler attached to the skull), the main beam's diameter and circumference were larger, sure signs of a buck being in its prime. I hunted hard for the buck the entire next hunting season and only once caught a brief glimpse of him. The buck's rack appeared to be slightly smaller than the year previous.

That winter, I again looked for the buck's sheds and found them within 200 yards of where its previous sheds had been found. Indeed, they were slightly smaller but still would have grossed in the 170s on the B&C scoring system. Interestingly, its mass was smaller than the year before. In comparing its beam circumference just above the burr to the pedicel attachment area, its beam circumference was slightly smaller than where the antler attached to the buck's head. With big antlers that have obviously come from a mature buck, this is usually an indication the buck is starting to show the effects of advanced aging.

Needless to say, the following fall I hunted the same area where the sheds had been found. In about the middle of the deer season, I spotted the buck from a distance and was able to stalk to within about 200 yards of it. From a solid rest I shot the deer with a .270. It fell in its tracks.

When I walked to where my buck lay, I was amazed by the beauty of its antlers, though now showing the effects of age and a rough-weather antler growing season. Even more amazing was that the buck fell within ten yards of where I had found its sheds the previous winter!

Thankfully, the buck had not gone downhill too much. The deer's main beams still measured nearly 27 inches long and the rack's longest point was more than 13 inches. All of its points were relatively long except the browtines, which were just barely an inch in length. Still this remains one of my favorite deer—and one that taught me the value of hunting close to where I found its shed antlers.

The same year I finally got that buck, I also shot a deer on another property I hunted on occasion, about 300 miles from there. During one of my wintertime, shed hunting, post-season scouting trips I had found the cast antlers of a buck lying side by side near the corner of the property. Each side of the rack had a split rear tine, like the dichotomous branching of a mule deer.

After taking the long-tined buck I shifted my hunting emphasis to the "double-branched" buck. Although I had seen bigger bucks on the property, this particular deer really piqued my interest. The first afternoon I was on the property, I set up a tripod deer stand within about 200 yards of where the sheds had been found. I hunted that same afternoon and watched four different bucks walk through the area.

The next morning I was in my tripod well before daylight. The rut was underway and bucks were on the move. Before 8:00 a.m., I passed up five good bucks including a young, wide ten-pointer. It was one of those perfect mornings, cool though not overly cold with high overcast skies and a light northerly wind blowing. Even better, the rut was just really starting to grasp the local whitetail herd within its fingers of fall madness.

I had stood up to stretch when I caught the movement of another buck. I saw its darkened tarsal glands and hocks before I saw its antlers. I knew whatever the buck's antlers were going to look like, this buck was certainly mature. This time, rather than raising my binocular for a better look, I raised my scoped rifle and peered at the movement behind the screen of brush. Moments later, the buck stepped out into an open lane. The first thing I noticed about its head was the massive antler rack. Both the back tines were forked like a mule deer. I simply slid the safety forward and when the crosshairs settled just behind the shoulder, I squeezed the trigger.

Moments later I stood admiring my handsome buck's rack. I could scarcely take my eyes off of the antlers, but when I did, I noticed that the buck had fallen less than ten steps from where I had picked up its sheds the previous winter.

On numerous other occasions, hunters on properties I manage have taken bucks within less than 100 yards of where I found the deer's shed antlers. I have also taken several other bucks extremely close to where we found their sheds the previous winter.

Are these fluke occurrences, or does finding shed antlers lead to taking good bucks? Decide for yourself. As for me, you'll see me hunting close to the area where I find impressive sheds!

I settled in my treestand and looked to the heavens as I said a little prayer and kindly asked to be blessed with a deer. I would soon learn prayers are answered.

On November 28, I climbed into my stand near Cape Girardeau, Missouri. Up to this point in my archery career, I had only arrowed a doe, but this season I had tried to take off early from work and hunt a couple hours each day for a buck. I have had

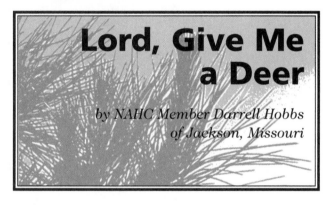

Lord, Give Me a Deer

by NAHC Member Darrell Hobbs
of Jackson, Missouri

good success while hunting with a firearm but was still learning about archery hunting.

About ten minutes after I said my prayer and settled in, I heard a noise in a thicket near me. Suddenly, a 100-pound-plus buck came toward the base of my tree. The only problem was that the buck was coming straight on, and I couldn't take a shot. Then the deer turned to one side and presented me with a perfect shot. I released my arrow and watched the deer dash off into the brush.

I climbed down out of the stand and headed home to tell my wife the good news. She returned later to help me look for the buck. As I looked for my arrow, Karen suddenly told me that I had bagged a nice ten pointer. That's when I really got excited.

My buck scored 146 Pope & Young and qualified for several other state record books. It had a 20-plus-inch inside antler spread and it field dressed at 185 pounds. Prayers do come true.

NAHC member Darrell Hobbs of Jackson, Missouri, proudly displays the 10-point whitetail buck he arrowed from his treestand.

Listen to the Woods

Blue jays and squirrels frequently sound an alarm if they see a hunter or deer. If you're hunting and hear them causing a ruckus, look in that direction to see what they are barking or squawking about.

Last Hunt with Dad

*by NAHC Life Member David Wallace
of Crystal River, Florida*

*O*n a cold January morning, I was planning another father and son hunting trip. Dad and I loaded all of our gear into the car and after eating a light lunch, we got our guns and headed out. We parked the car alongside the highway and started the long walk into the woods. The sun shone brightly, and the temperature was around 55 degrees. The walk was quiet; we just enjoyed being together. I had gotten permission from a friend to hunt on his property because I did not want to be disturbed by any other people on our trip into the woods.

The walk took a long time because we had to take it slow. When we finally arrived by the spring where the small creek ran out into the swamp, I picked out a good spot with plenty of sign and set him up in a chair. I told him to sit still and to keep his eyes open because I had seen quite a few hogs in this bottom a couple days earlier.

In the beginning of the season I had seen a nice buck in the same area. I left Dad there and moved farther into the woods to work my way around and try to drive something back by him. He had not yet taken his first deer and this trip would be the perfect time.

I pushed my way through the heavy brush for some time until I came to a small pine thicket. The sun had settled low on the horizon, and it would be dark soon. I knew that I could not be far from the spring, so I sat down and waited for darkness to come. The sun had just dropped below the treetops when a buck began to cross the pine thicket. Though I wanted Dad to be the one to take it, I was not going to let a legal buck pass by, so I slipped the safety off and readied myself for the shot.

As I waited for the buck to enter an opening, I heard Dad shout for me; of course, the deer was gone in a flash. There would be no meat for the freezer or trophy for the wall, but that's not what hunting is about. The smell of the damp earth, the warm sun shining on our faces, the time spent with family and friends— that's what we love.

When I worked my way over to where he was, Dad told me he was ready to go home. You see, he had been diagnosed with cancer four weeks earlier and was taking chemotherapy. He had been getting weaker by the day. After I helped him get his gear together, we started the long walk back to the car.

Now my favorite hunting partner is gone, and I miss my father very much.

The Beginnings of Barrels

Recorded history is unclear as to when the first firearm was invented. We know that it was probably a cannon. We also know that the Chinese developed the first form of gunpowder, but there is no record that they ever used it as a propellant to shoot anything out of a tube.

It's likely that firearms were a European idea, probably in the early 13th century, using the Chinese idea as a base. There are records of early cannon barrels being cast, but in the 1200s and 1300s, that was an expensive and slow process demanding skilled artisans and scarce metal.

Source: Shooter's Choice

White-Tailed Deer Quiz #1 Answers
(from pages 30-32)

1) False. Does occasionally grow antlers and a hunter somewhere brings an antlered doe to the check-in station each fall.

2) d. All of these glands help a deer produce antlers.

3) True. Early settlers called whitetails the Virginia deer and the species retains part of the name even though it inhabits many states in the United States.

4) True. Two hundred and fifty-pounders are common in Minnesota, and Wisconsin each hunting season and 300 pounds-plus deer have been recorded. One Minnesota monster weighed 511 pounds!

5) False. White-tailed deer in the deer's northern range in Canada can stand up to 40 inches tall but the average is 36 inches tall at the top of the shoulders or about even with the average man's belt buckle.

6) False.

7) True. Early settlers shipped deer hides back to Europe and paid bills with deer hides.

8) True. A deer can eat vegetation, and then later regurgitate the contents and chew a cud like a cow.

9) True. They also used fires to drive deer and sometimes herded the deer into a corral.

10) b. Rhode Island in 1646 passed a law prohibiting deer hunting.

11) a. The white spots help the fawn blend with small spots of sun that filter in through the forest's canopy.

12) a. There are more hairs per square inch on a deer in the summer.

13) True. In late summer a deer sheds its red coat and grows a brownish-gray-colored winter coat.This hair is shed in late winter and replaced with a reddish summer coat.

14) b. Albinos also have pink eyes.

15) c.

16) b.

17) True. They have been clocked at up to 30 mph.

18) False.

19) True. Generally a larger body mass is needed to survive colder temperatures.

20) a. Pedicels

21) True. Antlers are generally shed each winter and are regrown beginning each spring. They are the only bone that grows outside of a body.

22) b. A white-tailed deer's antlers beam curves forward.

23) b. A whitetail's antlers normally have single times protruding upward from the main beam. A mule deer's antlers seem to fork from forks.

24) b. The mule deer has a metatarsal gland nearly three inches long. The whitetail's metatarsal gland is about 1.5 inches long.

25) a. A mule deer has a black-tipped tail that is normally smaller than a whitetail's tail.

White-Tailed Deer Quiz #2 Answers
(from pages 53-54)

1) b. Antlers have to dry at least 60 days before they can be officially scored for the record books, according to Pope and Young and Boone and Crockett Club's guidelines. Antlers should be air dried and some shrinkage can be expected.

2) b. A very popular hunting destination, Montana offers some of the nation's largest elk, white-tailed deer, black bears and pronghorns. The state's vast wilderness areas are a dream come true for many hunters who go there.

3) a. A deer has hooves that are split. They make a heart-shaped print on the ground when a deer walks, with the point telling you the direction the deer traveled. The dew claws on a deer's leg normally only touch the ground when a deer is running, not while it's walking normally.

4) a. Antler development in most white-tailed bucks begins to decline as the deer reaches six and seven years of age. This decline is related to the deer's teeth wearing down and the deer being less efficient at eating.

5) d. All of these minerals are needed to grow antlers. Salt licks that some hunters put out do not provide many nutrients; hunters would be better off placing red-trace mineral salts for deer in areas where this is legal. Mineral salts are available at many farm supply centers.

6) b. In the 1970s, deer hunting gripped the nation in a big way. Before that time, some states were still stocking and transferring deer and some areas had struggling populations. Now, some areas have too many deer!

7) a. Alabama is the place to hunt if you take your deer hunting seriously since you can hunt there for more than three months of the year! Alabama is one southern state where early restocking programs used big-bodied whitetails from some northern states. A record book buck is possible there thanks to the reintroduced deer herd's genetics.

8) a. South Carolina—with its deer hunting season normally opening in August—has one of the earliest opening days in the nation. Take some bug spray if you go; the mosquitoes can be fierce.

9) a. With a population of more than ten million, our nation's hunters are a powerful economic force. Hunters spend millions on ammunition, firearms, archery gear, camping supplies, motel rooms, gas, meals and licenses. Hunters, not the general taxpaying public, support our nation's wildlife conservation efforts.

10) a. The antler rattling technique is normally recognized to have begun in Texas. Hunters in almost every region where the white-tailed deer lives now use this method to attract a buck during hunting season.

Who's Winning?

I was set up on a high ridge, overlooking patches of grass and trees. I was watching a path to my left. Just after sunrise, the air filled with the sounds of gunfire. I didn't see any sign of movement at all until sometime around 9:00 a.m. It was coming from below. Hunters who must have gotten tired of sitting were walking slowly down a path between a high grass patch and a tree patch. I decided to sit still and let them move the deer around, and take in some more of the view I had. About 9:30 a.m., I noticed a large-racked buck sneaking around the section of grass. Two does were circling around the other way. They suddenly stopped and started looking around. Then I saw the buck drop to its knees and crawl to the other side of the grass and slip into the brush. Four hunters walked right past him. They spotted one of the does about 100 yards away from them and started after her. About 15 minutes later, I spotted the buck sneaking out of the brush again and head off in the other direction. I thought to myself..."How embarrassing." Just then I noticed I was being watched from the path. She was a big doe, and looking right at me. I raised my shot gun and she took off. I sighted her in and gently squeezed the trigger...CLICK!!!...I had forgotten to chamber a slug! I couldn't help thinking..."Is someone watching me and thinking, HOW EMBARRASSING...?"

NAHC Member Vincent J. Cox,
Akron, Ohio

THE ADVENTURE OF BIG GAME

*E*lk hunting is a challenge no matter what equipment you choose to hunt with. Archery enthusiasts, in particular, are an elite group of hunters who relish the challenge of getting close. I know from personal experience that looking into the eyes of a screaming, slobbering, lusting 600- to 700-pound bull elk presents a thrilling adventure that deserves to be categorized in a class of its own. A close encounter with a 5x5 New Mexico bull elk a couple of years

Archery Elk at High Altitudes

by NAHC Member Kathy Butt of Portland, Tennessee

ago illustrates a prime example of how hunters can sometimes get a little too close for comfort.

I was hunting an 11,000-acre private ranch in northern New Mexico, a ranch my husband, Foster, and I have leased for the last several years. My first experiences with elk hunting were on this ranch during the rifle seasons, and I had been successful in taking a nice bull each of the three years I hunted. Archery hunting those big critters was going to be the ultimate challenge, and I thought I had a pretty good idea of just how tough it really could be.

I quickly discovered that chasing a bugling bull elk through dark timber at an elevation of 10,000-plus feet does terrible things to a Tennessee lowlander whose lungs are accustomed to a mere 200 feet above sea level. No one told me I'd have to pack a fire extinguisher to put out the fire in my lungs. And through personal experience, I've found that hunting in high altitudes challenges even the most physically prepared hunter. There's no doubt you can't prepare your lungs for hunting at 10,000 feet but you can prepare your muscles for miles of hiking in steep terrain. Preparing your physical body will save you days of agonizingly sore muscles.

Hunting gear has improved dramatically since my first encounter with a big—and I mean big—6x6 bull elk. Most of my archery hunting for elk is done in the dark timber, and, once I'd become intimately familiar with the ranch's terrain, I was comfortable with hunting solo. It was a challenge...and I thrive on challenges.

My hunt was the last week of New Mexico's archery season, and I'd just discovered several massive rubs and a wallow or two. Actually, it was the bugling of two rival bulls that led me into the area that a really big bull had claimed as his territory. Good luck just wasn't in the cards for me that day. But a week later, the last day of the season, it all came together.

The morning was perfect as I began hunting. Under a crisp, clear-blue sky, the bulls were talking. The bulls weren't just talking...they were hot! They were bugling insults back and forth, and I didn't have to make a single call. The big bull's bugling led me right into its area, and I was able to sneak in unannounced. The terrain was filled with waist-high elk bushes. (I don't know the correct name for those bushes, but the elk love to eat them.) Massive rubs were visible from every direction, and I backed up to a large spruce to break my outline and went to work.

The bow I carried was a used Darton Viper that my husband had purchased for me. Although a Darton Viper was an excellent bow for men, its 45-pound let-off and too-long draw length made it a difficult bow for me to draw and hold. There I was, backed up into the spruce and waiting for the screaming bull to appear.

After one short bugle and gruff-belly grunt from my mouth diaphragm, that bull came charging down the ridge I was standing on. My heart was pounding so furiously that I began to shake.

The author poses with the bull elk she arrowed at less than 30 yards after the animal almost stepped on her as her husband, Foster, called the big bull.

Even my bow began to shake, and it took a great deal of inner composure to calm down as I watched the bull trot down the ridge to my left. His head was low and swinging from side to side as the bull searched for the intruding bull he thought he had heard. Then the bull paused 40 yards out to bugle its challenge. The bull's eyes rolled back in his head, slobber dripped from his nostrils and his urine flew in all directions. This sight was almost more than my heart could take.

My knees were beginning to knock uncontrollably. I had to gain control of myself! It was a struggle to jerk my concentration back to reality. I had a crosswind that was blowing from my right to my left and the bull was steering to my left as he approached. I was going to be in trouble if this bull continued on his present course, so I drew my bow as the bull reached a triple-trunked aspen 15 yards ahead of me.

Precision Practice

One of the best ways to prepare for archery hunting season if you will be hunting from a treestand is to practice with a hunting buddy. To make practice more realistic, one hunter should get on stand wearing full hunting gear and a safety belt. This hunter stands facing the tree as the other hunter moves a foam McKenzie-type 3-D archery deer target to a location out from the stand.

The hunter on the ground then moves out of harm's way to the base of the tree and signals for the hunter on the stand to turn and take a shot. The hunter's first shot counts. The target should be located so that kneeling and sitting shots can be taken.

After a few sessions it's time to switch the hunter on stand with the ground crew. This is very realistic and useful practice just prior to archery deer season. Try to use the same type of terrain in which you'll be deer hunting. This practice also gives you a chance to try out all of your gear before opening day.

Big problem. I was at full draw when the bull took two steps down off the side of the ridge and stopped. All I could see was the top of his back and his back-scratcher rack. There I was at full draw, and I waited... and I waited... and waited... and then I struggled with the bow. A 45-pound let-off set to pull 50 pounds was just more than this little gal could hold for very long. The bull didn't know I was there until I tried unsuccessfully to let down without drawing the bull's attention. You guessed it. The bull caught my movement and whirled to escape back to the ridge. A quick bugle from me stopped him 40 yards out, but he just wasn't going to play this game any longer. The bull paused only to look back in curiosity, and that's when I got a real good look at the massive 350 class bull I'd come very close to arrowing. What a beauty!

Two seasons later I once again had a very close and personal encounter with another bull elk, a smaller 5x5 that wound up in my freezer and on the wall. This was possible thanks to me using the proper equipment, to my having more confidence in my abilities and to the expert calling tactics of my favorite hunting partner. On this particular hunt I was accompanied by my husband, Foster, who had filled his tag a day or two earlier with his bow. I was using a Golden Eagle Evolution bow that has been specifically designed to meet the needs of small-framed shooters. The bow offered a 65% let-off, a shorter draw length with a 39-inch axle-to-axle length, and it weighed less. It was much easier for me to hold at full draw and easier to pack around. It's one of the quietest and smoothest shooting bows I've ever used—an excellent bow for elk hunting.

That particular morning was another crisp, clear bluebird morning, and the bulls were bugling big time. Our problem was that the elk herd was on the other side of a volcanic flow, and it would take us some time to work our way around to where we knew they were feeding. Our plan was to intercept them before they headed up and over the rocky ridge to bed in dark timber. Foster knew exactly where those elk were feeding, but we hadn't heard any cow or bull talk for the last few minutes. Foster stopped periodically to pull handfuls of grass along the way. He knew we were closing in, and he was expecting to see the herd at any moment, so he wanted to cover our approach by sounding like elk feeding. An excellent tactic I'll remember for future hunts!

Just before cresting the hill, Foster motioned for me to work my way up the trail and choose a set-up spot to the right. He was going to set up approximately 25 yards to my left and try to call the elk up the trail with cow talk. This would also focus their attention in his direction and not mine. The problem was that I worked my way along up the trail a little too far and was in the open when I spotted the herd just below the crest of the ridge about 50 yards below. Luckily, I saw them before they had a chance to see me. I just couldn't move but was able to go down on one knee without getting caught.

They were just too darn close to make another move. I managed to slip an arrow out of my quiver and nock it, adjust my face mask and nod to Foster that I was ready for whatever was about to happen. Foster had brought along the video camera and was filming the herd, which consisted of two 5x5 bulls and a dozen or so cows. The smaller of the two bulls was busy raking an aspen 50 yards away and picked his head up to look in our direction when Foster issued the first cow call. A couple more cow calls piqued the bull's curiosity, and he responded by walking straight up the trail to me, not to Foster.

On this trip I found out that it doesn't take a long-legged bull very long to cover 40 yards. I was down on one knee with nothing between the bull and me but my bow. I felt small—very small! My heart was pounding so furiously, I could barely hear Foster as he issued a shrill bugle in an effort to turn the bull toward him. The bugle merely stopped the bull momentarily.

The 5x5 was ten yards and approaching. I would be lying if I said I was calm, cool and collected. But I did have a plan. This was where knowing your guide personally and knowing how he reacts in situations like this can swing things in your direction. After hunting with him for 15 years, I had every faith in Foster's guiding expertise.

When the bull stood head-on at five yards, and I realized he wasn't going to change his course, I drew my bow and held. Of course, the bull bolted in the other direction, but I held at full draw and followed his movement, hoping Foster would bugle and stop the bull within shooting range. And he did! Foster's bugle stopped the bull at 27 yards and at a quartering away angle. I quickly estimated the yardage and placed my single fluorescent sight pin low and behind the bull's front shoulder, releasing my 2114 Easton Super Slam arrow tipped with a 120-grain Vortex broadhead. The arrow connected with a resounding thud, and I watched as the bull bolted, stopped and stumbled at the edge of the timber.

Foster had gotten the entire scenario on film, and I was trying to regain my composure when he finally walked down to where I was still kneeling. The bull was hit a little lower than I would have liked, and we needed to give him time to go down. He wouldn't go far, and I sure didn't want to push him.

A few hours later we recovered my first archery elk, a nice 5x5 bull. Not as big as the 350-class bull I had called in previously, but what a thrilling experience! Any elk taken with archery equipment is a good elk. Bull or cow, they're all challenging.

My using the proper equipment and having a few years of elk hunting experience tucked under my belt certainly were vital in my archery hunting success.

Easy Arrows

Here are a few suggestions for making your arrows easier to remove from your practice target:

- apply a coat of car wax to them just as you would your truck or automobile
- apply a coat of cooking spray to your arrows
- rub carbon arrows with wax paraffin

Predators Quiz
See page 160 for the correct answers.

1. True or false? Wolves are cousins to coyotes but can be two to three times larger and have shorter ears.

2. Which animal is considered to be an omnivore?
   a. bear
   b. coyote
   c. fox
   d. all of the above

3. True or false? The pupils of a red fox's eyes are elliptical, similar to those of a house cat.

4. True or false? Coyotes tend to be solitary animals with the female raising her pups alone.

5. The principal food of the timber wolf is:
   a. ptarmigan
   b. bears
   c. rats and moles
   d. deer and moose

6. Which three wildcats can be found in the wild in the contiguous 48 states?
   a. lions, bobcats and lynx
   b. lynx, bobcats and cougars
   c. cougars, bobcats and nilgia
   d. none of the above

7. True or false? The bobcat can be easily identified by the feather-like tufts above its ears.

8. The Latin name for the red fox is:
   a. *Vulpes vulpes*
   b. *Felis rufus*
   c. *Canis lupus*
   d. all of the above

I grew up in the central part of Pennsylvania where game animals and birds are still very abundant. We saw deer and turkey almost every day. My younger brother decided to purchase a 60-acre tract of mountain land that bordered our family's 110-acre farm. After my brother bought it, he decided that he wanted to harvest the mature timber that was standing. At that time I was working as a procurement forester for a local timber company, so he

Yes, Dad, I Saw a Bear!

by NAHC Life Member Jim Temchack of Orrtanna, Pennsylvania

asked me to handle the sale. While I was cruising the timber and marking and recording all the timber to be removed during harvest, something happened to me that I will never forget...

I had already finished cruising four lines and was deep on the backside of the tract, working my way forward toward the opposite boundary line and my truck. I was following my compass bearing due south, when it happened: Off to my right in a small ravine I heard a loud, nerve-shattering noise. It sounded like trees and laurel were being uprooted and thrown everywhere. It kept moving forward; I froze! The crashing noise started at the top of the ravine and continued until it finally came to a dead stop in the deep hollow below. I saw nothing. The only sound I could hear was my own heart pounding forcefully. What could have caused that terrible clamor so deep in this quiet and peaceful forest? Everything was now quiet and calm. I waited for about two minutes—which seemed like two hours—and decided to continue on my southward journey.

Soon I reached a point where I needed to take another compass sighting. As I lifted my compass up to eye level and was sighting downhill, there, straight in front of me—due south—was the source of all that noise I had heard above—a large black bear! I froze. It was on all fours, not moving but sniffing and pawing the ground around it. The huge bear hadn't seen me yet. I was too far down the hill to retreat, and I knew better than to run. I just stood there, watching one of nature's true wonders in its natural state and environment. The bear was beautiful. I watched it for at least 5 minutes, becoming lost in true amazement. When I finally came back to reality, I thought, now what? The bear still hadn't noticed I was standing there, invading its territory just as it was invading my due south compass bearing. I decided that it was time to make my presence known, but in a calm, subtle way so as not to disturb it too much. I made a low but audible sound with my voice. Nothing happened. The second time I made the sound, the bear responded. It stood up on its hind legs and looked my way. At that point, I didn't know who was more startled, the bear or me! It looked at me, sniffed the cold air and took off running. And of course it ran—you guessed it—due south.

Now what? I sat down and tried to gather my thoughts about what had just happened and what I would do next. Should I continue due south or offset my compass line? After about ten minutes of careful pondering, I decided to continue due south.

Once my legs finally agreed and decided it was safe to move again, I continued to the bottom of the hollow. I stopped and studied the ground that the bear had been pawing when I first saw it. Looking back up the small ravine, I could easily tell the path the bear had followed en route to the hollow and to the spot where I now stood. It didn't matter wheather the bear was male or female—all I know is that my hand fit well within the outline of the bear's paw print.

Since it was getting late, I decided to continue on. Making my way through the heavy underbrush of mountain laurel and rhododendron, I continued to find broken limbs and disturbed leaves, telling me that the bear had headed in the same exact direction. I continued pacing and taking sample timber plots, but it was hard to concentrate on what I was doing. I expected to see the bear up in front of me in the heavy mountain laurel at anytime. Had it had lunch yet? At a point close to the property boundary line, the bear took a detour from the due south bearing we had both been sharing toward the top of the mountain. Finally, and thankfully, reaching my destination, I went to my truck and headed home.

That evening, I told my father of my experience. I can still see the look of total surprise and disbelief on his face. Soon, after he had finished laughing, he told me all the stories and rumors he had heard from farmers all over the valley. A large bear, they believed, was destroying corn crops throughout the valleys on both sides of the mountain. No one had ever seen the bear or knew where it lived. The bear was a true local legend, and I had seen it first!

At special times, when I'm by myself, hunting, hiking or fishing, I think of my run-in with the bear and laugh to myself. I know that something special had happened to me that day—something very few people are lucky enough to experience in a lifetime. I also think of my father, who has since passed away. I think of the special look and expression he had on his face after hearing my story. I just smile, look toward the sky and say, "Yes, Dad, there are bears in those hills!"

Bear Quiz

See pages 160-161 for the correct answers.

1. True or false? Typically, black bear sows will deliver five or six cubs a year.

2. While the most common color of a black bear is black, they can also be what other colors?
   A. reddish brown
   B. blond
   C. cinnamon
   D. all of the above

3. The Latin for the common black bear is:
   A. *Ursus horribilis*
   B. *Ursus americanus*
   C. *Ursus carnivora*
   D. all of the above

4. True or false? Black bear are more active than normal during a light rain.

5. Typically, the black bear's peak breeding season is in:
   A. September and October
   B. June and July
   C. January and February
   D. November and December

6. True or false? Black bear are entirely carnivorous.

7. True or false? The sex of a bear can be determined by the coloration of its snout. Males have a darker snout than females.

8. The male black bear is typically called a:
   A. sow
   B. boar
   C. bear
   D. none of the above

9. What species of bear has killed the greatest number of humans within the last 200 years?
   A. black bear
   B. polar bear
   C. grizzly bear
   D. Kodiak bear

10. True or false? Black bear reproduce through a process called delayed implantation, where the fertilized egg does not immediately begin to develop.

11. For a thick, full coat, the best time to hunt back blear is:
    A. during the dead of winter
    B. June and July
    C. in the spring
    D. all of the above

12. A portion of a polar bear's diet consists of which of the following:
    A. kelp
    B. seals
    C. beluga whales
    D. all of the above

The Hunt Lives On

When 70 youngsters were given the choice between participating in the National Elk Refuge's youth elk hunt near Jackson, Wyoming, or a $1,000 mountain bike offered by the Fund for Animals, all 70 youngsters chose the elk hunt.

The anti-hunting group tried to entice each of the 12- to 17-year-olds with the bike if they would turn in their refuge permit and promise not to hunt during the rest of the year. Several of the kids cited the role of the the hunter in wildlife management as the reason the youth elk hunt was more important than a new bike.

The youth hunt is traditionally offered on the opening two days of the refuge season. Younger hunters have had this chance to participate since the Wyoming legislature lowered the minimum big game hunting age from 14 to 12.

The north portion of the elk refuge is open to elk hunting by special permit. The objective number of elk to winter on the refuge is 7,500, and the herd needs to be trimmed to capacity annually.

Pronghorn Tip

When hunting pronghorns, you should be out scouting during the final hour of daylight. Where you see the pronghorns as dark approaches is generally where they will be the next morning. They bed down and stay put for the night unless disturbed by a predator or hunter. Return to the area early the next morning and approach the location quietly from downwind. This strategy will greatly increase your chances for success.

*G*osh, hanging in the meat locker, it was as large as me. My guide was excited, and the owner was too. I just wanted to have my picture taken and get the meat to the processing plant.

Both the owner and the guide told me it was the largest Russian boar that had been taken from the preserve since they opened almost 12 years earlier. The preserve covered more than 275 acres, was fully fenced and included nearly 60 acres of swampland.

Don't Let the Hogs Catch You Down

*by NAHC Life Member John Caknipe
of Chase City, Virginia*

The owner's primary purpose in opening the preserve was to use a former sheep pasture that had been fenced with woven wire. The owner and several friends thought it would be a good idea to have a few wild hogs for some weekend fun. Of course, after six years the fun was gone and the hogs began to multiply without disruption from hunters.

After three years of little hunting pressure, the owner decided to cash in on his bountiful supply of wild pork. He secured a license as a wildlife preserve. I was there hunting during the fourth week after he had opened. This was the prime time; in the three weeks preceding my hunt there had been only 12 other hunters.

When I arrived at the lodge the evening before the hunt, the guide, owner and two other hunters and I sat around planning the strategy for the next day. During our talk, the owner told us that we should be very careful. He stated that after the first week of hunting they began to find small pigs dead. He went on to say that the small pigs had been savagely attacked, apparently by an old rogue boar. However, no one had seen the boss boar thus far.

In any event, he was sending a guide with each of us. The guide was more for protection and backup than actually guiding. The next day would prove to be exciting and I was primed for it.

Next morning we were awakened at 5:00 a.m. Now, I'm not a morning person so six cups of coffee later made me ready for breakfast: three more cups of coffee, plus bacon, eggs and pancakes. Now it was time to go hunting.

At my side I had a canteen full of coffee for the morning walk. A few cookies in my pocket rounded out the morning break. The coffee was just beginning to kick in when I saw movement.

Straight ahead of me were about six or seven pigs. I used my binocular and determined they were all little ones. From there I began hunting the ridge areas. I moved slowly and deliberately.

The owner had said that he believed there were between 50 and 60 pigs on the preserve. I saw a lot, but all of them were little ones. By midmorning, it was time for a coffee break. I finished off my canteen.

Then I went to the stalk. This was one of those days of "fun hunting." I was there with my holstered .44 Virginia Dragoon pistol. (Just call me Wyatt or Jesse, if you like.) I was ready for the quick draw and the showdown at the "OK Preserve."

Moving from the ridges into clusters of young pine trees, I began to see more movement. I was crawling along low to see under the pines, but all I could make out were legs—no heads were visible.

Soon it was time for lunch. During lunch, everyone was cheerful, although no hunter had shot any pork. All of us had seen several, but none of the pigs were the size we wanted. Actually, one hunter did see a big one, but he froze. The guide said that hunter just stood there with the boar 15 yards away and could not pull the trigger. The hunter confessed that this was the first time he had ever been hunting and that he had never shot his .30-06. Unbelievable!

After lunch, I went back to the hunt. My guide suggested that we hunt the swamps. The other two hunters had seen nothing in them that morning, but maybe they would push something in the afternoon. My guide would walk around one side of each of the small areas and make a lot of noise. I would walk the other side as quietly as I could.

After pushing the third swamp area, I began to feel an over-whelming sensation. I realized I had drunk about 20 cups of coffee without any relief. It was time to go, and I mean now!

Here I was, in the middle of a 15-acre swamp, and I had to undo my coveralls and relieve myself—urgently. No sooner had I started the relieving process when I heard a terrible noise. There was growling, grunting, brush breaking and stomping on the ground nearby. I thought it might be my guide, but when I looked up I saw a monster heading straight for me! This was the only trail in the swamp and I was standing in the middle of it.

So what did I do? I pulled my coveralls aside, drew my pistol and fired a hip shot. That big old hog hit the ground. I holstered my pistol so I could finish what I had started, but then that ole hog jumped up and headed straight for me. This time there was determination in its face. I drew and fired again while it was about 15 yards away.

Down the hog went. I stood there, took aim and waited. Sure enough, it got up a third time, and I fired. I hit it right in the head; this time it was down for good.

My guide came running to my location. I wheeled around thinking it might be another hog, and he just burst out laughing.

It was a strange sight to see a hunter standing in the middle of the swamp, holding a smoking .44 Magnum pistol, with his bib overalls around his knees and a huge hog lying within ten yards.

Venison Backstrap Kabob

venison backstrap
onions
bell peppers
tomatoes
fresh mushrooms
Italian salad dressing

Marinade:
¼ cup soy sauce
¼ cup teriyaki sauce
Tobasco sauce for spicy flavor

Slice whole backstrap ½-inch thick across the grain.
Marinate in soysauce and teriyaki sauce for at least
1 hour. Slice up onions, bell peppers (red, yellow and
green varieties for color) and slightly green tomatoes.
Alternately slide meat, veggies and mushroom caps on
skewers and cook slowly on outdoor grill or rotisserie.
Baste with Italian salad dressing.

Dennis Hoddy
Ponca City, OK

As my daughter, Heidi, and I neared a swampy meadow that crisp, frosty morning, I heard it! We stopped instantly, nodded to each other, acknowledging that both of us weren't hallucinating and I whispered, "It's a bull. Let's get to the meadow." We quickly sneaked into a spot just inside the meadow with visibility in the direction of the grunt sound. I gave the most seductive cow call that I could come up with. We were rewarded with music to a moose

A Mom and a Moose

by NAHC Member Judy Maida of Prince George, British Columbia

caller's ears—a quick audible response. Actually, in the next few seconds, all pandemonium broke loose! Not just one, but three bulls enthusiastically responded. Wow, and did they respond! Nature's chess game had begun.

At daybreak that brisk late September morning, we had hurried out of our camp and driven to one of my favorite nearby hunting spots in north-central British Columbia. We began to walk toward the steep, timbered mountain slope and to our moose stand. The previous day, however, my 23-year-old daughter and I had hunted hard in a nearby area but had found no rutting moose sign. Today was obviously a different story. My big bull tag had been waiting for this time to arrive!

Heidi had never been with me in a situation quite like this one. Her involvement in athletics and college had left precious little time for hunting. We were clearly in the middle of major rut activity and a moose hunter's dream.

The bull we had heard initially responded immediately and continuously. Its location seemed to be at the far end of the meadow, possibly on the hillside where we were originally headed—some 500 yards away. The bull sounded like a large, mature one. One of the other bulls sounded younger and desperate, almost unbull-like at times, calling nonstop and using every technique from grunts to high-pitched, almost obscene, "please, come to me" yearnings. This bull was some 400 yards to the left and behind our location, out of sight. The third bull gave just one single, deep grunt from behind our location, out of sight, somewhere to the right in the large, green timber. With all of the verbalization going on from the other two bulls, the exact location of the third bull was difficult to pinpoint.

A bull moose operetta, I thought. I am sure they were even harmonizing!

All of this rut frenzy lasted for what seemed to be an eternity, but it was probably only a few minutes. My daughter and I stood sharing the unfolding drama. As we listened, it became obvious that a cow had moved to one of the bulls, or perhaps she had been there from the beginning. The bull's first low grunt was meant for the cow.

The bulls were slowly moving toward the top of the mountain. I decided to make a move. We walked out of the meadow back to our original trail and headed toward the first bull's general direction. When Heidi inquired about any walking noise possible scaring these elusive beasts, I indicated that our movement might even help the situation. Movement sometimes stirs things up and causes action at rut time. There was virtually no air movement so it was unlikely any of the bulls would wind us. As it turned out, we didn't get to see the bull and cow since they moved out of the area.

At this point, we decided to try for one of the other bulls. As we neared the half-way mark on the trail toward the meadow where I had called, we heard a hair-raising grunt behind us. In fact, Heidi looked back in anticipation, half-expecting the bull to be breathing

*NAHC member Judy Maida of Prince George, British Columbia, with her
bull moose. Judy was hunting with her daughter at her side when she
downed the moose from 350 yards.*

down her neck! If I remember correctly, my daughter said it was more like the moose was in the same location as her fanny pack!

The bull thought we were the meandering cow from the meadow. We knelt down, and I chose a perfect shooting lane in hopes that it would appear any second. Well, the bull didn't. It is amazing what good ventriloquists bull moose can be. The bull quit grunting and was absolutely silent. So, back to the meadow we went to further entice him into the open and where I wanted him. It was nature's chess game—you make your move, I'll make mine.

I gave a cow call and quickly moved to where my daughter was hidden in the tall meadow grass. The bull responded beautifully as it smashed and crashed through 15-foot-tall willows like a freight train. All of this commotion brought an instant response from one of the other bulls. The second moose was not grunting with masculine, lowered tones. It was a back and forth verbal duel between the two.

After controlling my irregular heart beat, I stood poised to shoot. We waited in anticipation, as Heidi whispered, "Mom, there he is." Yes, there was a bull moose 350 yards away, at the far end of the meadow, throwing willows from side to side with its large golden paddles. All we could see facing us were the bull's head and horns as it stood in the bog between thick willows.

This was not the shot I wanted at that distance, so I waited. I wondered if the moose would make his move straight down the length of the meadow toward my calling. Instead, the bull turned 90 degrees to his right and stomped quickly and deliberately through the bog until he was hidden by sporadic willows at the meadow's edge. It became apparent that this was a bull on a mission! It seemed that this bull's strategy was to circle us.

I contemplated my next strategy as I watched through my scope. I found an opening in the willows in anticipation of seeing the bull's left shoulder. When the bull entered that point, I squeezed the trigger on my .30-06 rifle. The big bull spun explosively around 180 degrees and ran like a thoroughbred down his backtrail. On my second shot, the bull twirled completely around again, then raced forward on his original path. Then he turned straight away from us through the willows and toward the green timber. Then the bull disappeared. The moment certainly was an adrenaline rush for my daughter and me!

We walked down the meadow and around the water and bogs. This place was a moose's paradise. As we approached the spot where we had last seen the big bull, I was looking well ahead into the large green timber envisioning a moose peering at us or jumping to its feet. My gaze was broken by Heidi excitedly whispering, "There he is, there he is, Mom!" The bull was there all right, an awesome dark mass of rippling muscle. My bull was down for good. We could now see how truly magnificent this huge bull really was.

I saw the flash of pride in my daughter's eyes. It was a temporary role reversal where daughter praises mother. In an instant, the hunt itself became insignificant and that magical moment is forever ingrained in my mind.

Heidi mentioned how perfect this had all turned out. As the sun broke over the mountains and the beauty of morning's mist rose lazily from the meadow, we reflected on each detail of the morning's events, as though our minds feared we might someday forget. This would be Heidi's story to tell of the strategy, suspense and drama of this day's hunt.

Women Hunters Numbers Increasing

The number of women who hunt increases each year. The continuing increase is partly due to the Becoming An Outdoors-Woman (BOW) Course, offered by 44 states and nearly every Canadian province. More than 10,000 women have attended the courses that teach trapping, game cleaning, game calling and more. Contact your state's game department to locate a course near you. NAHC is a national BOW sponsor.

Choose the Correct Clothes

Choose your camouflage clothing to match the conditions you'll be hunting in. Today's camouflage patterns are very terrain specific. If you'll be in a treestand against a tree trunk, a treebark pattern might be your best choice. For early fall season and late spring hunting seasons, use patterns that are predominately green. Waterfowl hunters have marsh reed patterns to help them avoid detection from a duck's keen eyes.

Most game animals scan their environment to look for anything out of the ordinary, such as solid colors in large patterns. Animals also key in on movement. Camouflaging your face and hands while hunting will help make you less noticeable to your quarry.

Bowhunters need silence to be successful. An archer's wardrobe should be fleece and chamois. Avoid scratchy fabrics that make noise—even in your footwear.

Upland bird hunters still find that Cordura-faced garments are able to withstand piercing briers. If you choose to wear gloves while pheasant or grouse hunting, make sure the gloves do not prevent safe and easy firearm operation. No camouflage or protective clothing is useful if you can't fire your gun or shoot your bow.

I have a passion for sheep hunting. I had already completed my grand slam and needed to fulfill my desire for my fifth North American prized sheep species—a California bighorn.

After speaking several times with outfitter Bruce Ambler, I was convinced that he would provide me with an exceptional hunt. I decided to book with him.

Getting ready for the physical demands of the hunt required me to be in top condi-

High Mountain Bighorn Hunt

by NAHC Member Dan Amatuzzo
of Highland Mills, New York

tion. I arrived at Kamloops, British Columbia, and met Bruce. The next day we traveled to the base camp, an old miner's camp. There I also met Ken, our camp cook. At a spry 78-years-young, the way Ken chopped wood for the next two weeks would put most of us to shame. (He was also a great cook.)

For the next five days, on both a Honda four-wheeler and on horseback, we scoured the mountains. Bruce was trying to acclimate me to the six-and seven-thousand-feet elevations. We saw ewes and lambs while we hunted but no rams.

Next, Bruce decided that we should set out for his spike camp. We loaded camp onto horses with panniers and set out on a six-hour trek through some of the most beautiful mountains on Earth. Four hours into our trip, as we were coming down the side of a mountain, Bruce spotted a ram feeding on the opposite mountain, above timberline.

Bruce pulled out his spotting scope and glassed the ram for a long time. Then he suddenly announced that we should sneak away without spooking the ram, reassuring me that the ram would not leave. We quietly moved away unseen and made it to spike camp at 6:30 p.m.

After setting up camp, Bruce cooked a fantastic meal, and we slipped into our sleeping bags. Again, he reassured me that the ram would be there in the morning.

At 6:30 in the morning we left camp and spotted the ram where he had been feeding the night before. This time we were just below him in the scrub pine while he was above timberline. Once more, Bruce inspected the ram with his scope. The ram's horns looked like a full curl. Still being cautious and supportive, and also considering the great distance to the ram, Bruce once again reassured me that the ram was not alarmed and that he would remain in the area. Keep in mind that while we were hunting, only a full curl was permitted. Any wrong decision on Bruce's part could be trouble for him and me.

This spotting and surveying of the ram continued for the next two days. Finally, on Saturday, the season changed, which meant 3/4 curl or better was now legal. Bruce told me not to worry. He said the ram would stay in the area since we had not spooked it.

On this day, Bruce decided that we should stalk the ram from the other side of the mountain. At 6:30 a.m. we began walking. We walked and walked and walked; up mountains, down mountains, around mountains, through shale, beside boulders and over slippery serpentine rock. We walked through the most incredible places on earth. By the end of the day we had seen no sheep, no rams, no ewes and no lambs. Nothing. Bruce continued to assure me that we would find a ram.

We were ready to hunt again at 6:30 the next morning. This time Bruce proclaimed that we should go to the original place. Off we went to where we had previously spotted the ram. When we

NAHC member Dan Amatuzzo of Highland Mills, New York, found that pre-hunt physical conditioning helped him fill his bighorn tag.

couldn't find a ram, Bruce declared that the ram must have gone around to the other side of the mountain. Off we went, after tying up the horses in the timber. As we cleared the next drainage swale, there was the ram feeding 300 or 400 yards ahead of us. Through another swale we went, but trying to climb the side was too noisy. Bruce decided we should go down through the timber and approach the ram's location from the bottom. It was possible that an upward shot could prove advantageous.

Down we went, 1,000 feet into the timber. We found the timber to be too thick to maneuver through. Bruce looked at me and said, "We have to climb above him." You can only guess what I was about to tell him! But again, Bruce uttered those inspiring words, "He's ours." So up we went, on the side of the swale we couldn't climb before.

After about 40 minutes, Bruce said that we should be above the ram. We went about 40 or 50 yards around the mountainside, and, lo and behold, there the bighorn was below us—not more than 150 yards away. As we crawled, there were two large boulders between the sheep and us, and the ram was bedded down facing away from us.

Bruce set up his backpack as a bench rest. It was then that the most enjoyable hunt of my life with a splendid guide, outfitter and personal friend came to an end with a full curl ram.

Saw is a Simple Solution

To open the pelvis on any big game animal, use a dry wall saw to cut through the bone. This saw will also work great on any big game animal's chest. Much safer than a knife for these uses, a dry wall saw costs less than $10 and has replacement blades. You will also find uses for the saw in camp and at your hunting stand.

On a beautiful sunny day in Springer, New Mexico, my son, Seth, and I watch several pronghorn bucks. They are quite a distance away, and Seth asks me to tell him again how "easy" this hunt is going to be. You see, at the moment, they are out of gun range, as they have been all day. Now, as I try to tell my 12-year-old son to be patient, I am also amazed. Since they are always standing beside the road or just inside the fence, I thought

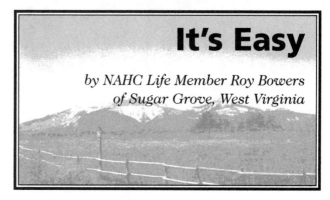

It's Easy

by NAHC Life Member Roy Bowers of Sugar Grove, West Virginia

pronghorns would be easy animals to hunt.

I hunt every year, and when I start packing my bags, my son begs to go with me. I had always felt that he was too young to hunt in the places I usually go. I always told him he could not go until he was of age, or until he had passed the hunter safety course. When the course became available in our area last summer, Seth asked his mother if she would take the course with him. He passed the course with the highest score in the class. In December, he also became a North American Hunting Club Life Member.

I thought a pronghorn hunt would be an easy hunt to take him on. I did some research and decided to give Tomahawk Outfitters owners Jim and Patty Kneip a

NAHC Life Member Seth Bowers (left) and his dad, Roy, with a pronghorn they tagged with a muzzleloader.

call. They impressed me from the first time I spoke with them. When I hunted mountain lion in Patagonia, Arizona, last summer, I decided to drive to Springer to see the Kneips. They were a delight to meet, and I knew this was the place to bring my son in the fall.

We flew from our home in Sugar Grove, West Virginia, to Albuquerque, New Mexico. My longtime hunting buddy, Harlan Mitchell, his son Jeff, and Richard Whitmore accompanied us. We saw several large pronghorns on the way in to the Kneips'. Seth was really excited; this was going to be easy.

Up early the next morning, we were all anxious to go bag our bucks. Seth could not keep still and said that he already had tabs on the largest one. We dropped the others off at different places on the ranch before Seth and I began our hunt together with Steve, our guide. As the morning went by, Seth shot at several pronghorns but was always too far away. He seemed to be getting disappointed. We could not get close enough to get a good shot; everything was at least

300 to 400 yards away. Several pronghorns worked their way to us and one nice buck came within 130 yards of where we sat. I motioned for Seth to shoot, but he insisted I take the shot. I motioned for Seth to shoot but he insisted I take the shot. It was a beautiful buck, and Steve felt it would book with the Longhunter Society. After taking care of my antelope we took Seth out again.

After seeing several more pronghorns —but none within gun range—we moved to a different location and noticed several feeding in our direction. When a nice buck walked within 140 yards of us, I asked Seth if he was close enough for a shot. He thought he was. "But Dad," he said, "I don't have any more shells with me." The truck was too far away, and the pronghorn was standing broadside. I asked him if he wanted to shoot my muzzleloader. Looking at me and at the buck, Seth nodded his head. I loaded my gun and handed it to him; he aimed the gun and fired. I think he started running to the pronghorn before it ever hit the ground! I'm so glad he is hunting with me now; watching the excitement on his face made the hunt even better for me.

We took some pictures and loaded his pronghorn into the truck. On our way back to camp, I asked Seth why he hadn't had any more shells with him. He exclaimed, "Dad, you said this was going to be an easy hunt!"

Back at camp, we learned that everyone had bagged a pronghorn. James looked at our pronghorn and felt that both animals would book. We spent the evening listening to Seth tell his hunting story. (He is almost as good as the rest of us!)

The following morning we drove to Eagle's Nest to look at Tomahawk's elk camp. We saw a lot of elk and some mule deer. We hope to go elk hunting with the Kneips soon. They are a first-class outfit and the food was wonderful.

On the flight back home, Seth already began planning the next hunt. "Dad, let's go caribou hunting in Alaska," he said. "They have to be easier to hunt than pronghorns!"

Pronghorn Quiz
How Much Do You Really Know
About the All-American Big Game Animal?

by NAHC Staff Member Tom Carpenter
See pages 161-163 for the correct answers.

The pronghorn antelope (*Antilocapra americana*) tests hunters' patience, stalking skills and marksmanship on the plains and prairies of North America. But how much do you really know about this fascinating, fun-to-hunt animal? Take this *Hunting Camp Lore* quiz and find out.

1. The pronghorn's closest relative on the evolutionary tree is the:
    a. mule deer
    b. elk
    c. mountain goat
    d. impala
    e. none of the above

2. The proper name for this beautiful prairie animal is:
    a. pronghorn
    b. antelope
    c. cabree
    d. a and b
    e. a, b and c

3. True or false? The pronghorn is the fastest animal on earth.

4. The month that sees the most pronghorn rutting and action is:
    a. August
    b. September
    c. October
    d. November

5. In the rutting season, a mature buck pronghorn prefers to defend:
    a. a harem of does
    b. a territory where does reside
    c. his honor and rank

6. True or false? Pronghorn bucks don't fight like whitetail or mule deer bucks do in the rut.

7. Across their range, the most important pronghorn foods, in order of importance, are:
   a. shrubs such as bitterbrush and sage, forbs, grasses
   b. forbs, shrubs, grasses
   c. grasses, forbs, shrubs
   d. grasses, shrubs, forbs

8. True or false? Pronghorn can get by on the water they get from the plants they eat and don't really need standing water.

9. The average live weight of a mature buck pronghorn is between:
   a. 80 and 100 pounds
   b. 101 and 120 pounds
   c. 121 and 140 pounds

10. If a pronghorn wants to feel safe, it will:
    a. hunker down under a sage bush to hide
    b. head to a flat, wide open expanse and stand in the middle of it
    c. head for the hills and rough country
    d. a or c
    e. b or c

11. In which state do hunters harvest the most pronghorns each year?
    a. Colorado
    b. Wyoming
    c. Montana
    d. South Dakota

12. The best rifle caliber for pronghorn hunting is:
    a. .270
    b. 243
    c. .30-06
    d. 7mm Mag.

13. True or false? Pronghorns jump fences easily and roam freely over the range.

14. True or false? Unlike a whitetail, who likes to stay at home, a pronghorn is a random roamer who never really settles in to a territory and pattern.

15. Which of these archery hunting methods sees the most pronghorns harvested each fall?
    a. decoying
    b. spot-and-stalk
    c. waterhole blinds
    e. still-hunting

16. True or false? Unlike the bison, which came close to extinction, pronghorns were never in such extreme danger.

17. True or false? Pronghorns running with their mouths agape are tiring out and ready to slow down.

18. Here's your essay question. Why are pronghorns so incredibly fast (more than twice as fast as their major predators), along with having such great endurance?

Here's NAHC Member Ron Bahls with a nice
Wyoming pronghorn buck. Note the sagebrush,
which is an essential of prime pronghorn habitat.

“Say Pete, you owe me a hundred bucks!” I sort of smiled and my friend of ten minutes continued. “I killed a big moose about a mile down the valley and you're going to get a grizzly off of him.” In about ten minutes he and his pals tossed their duffel into the Twin Beach that we had just come in on and were taking off from a beautiful little lake in the Logan Mountains of the Yukon. As we stood there on the shore I was reminded of Robert Service and his Yukon poems.

A Yukon Hunt

by L.D. “Pete” Peterzen
of Golden Valley, Minnesota

I've stood in some mighty-mouthed hollow
That's plumb-full of hush to the brim;
I've watched the big, husky sun wallow
In crimson and gold grow dim.

Three days earlier four of us had left Minneapolis, driving straight through to Grande Prairie, Alberta. The next morning we continued into Dawson Creek, British Columbia. After a hearty breakfast we took pictures of Mile Post 1 and then headed up the famous AlCan Highway, which was built during the Second World War to connect Alaska with the Lower 48. The highway was all that we had expected...a gravel road winding up and down through some very beautiful wild country. In one day we saw a young stone sheep, a young bull moose and a mature timber wolf. Another day brought us into Watson Lake, Yukon Territory. After taking pictures of the famous fence of sign posts from all over the world, we looked up our outfitter, Gordon Toole. Gordy had guided the author Clyde Ormond and was well recommended to us. Rightly so!

The next morning we loaded into a Twin Beach and flew out. In about an hour we were shaking hands with the fellow who had shot the moose. We cut cards to see who was going to guide

Illustration by Jeff Boehler

whom and I got the young guide who, at the time, was out bringing in the horses. Later, at dusk he came in riding and pushing the horses to the corral. "WHERE'S MY HUNTER?" he yelled. "Here," I answered. "Get your rifle, there's a grizzly on a dead moose back down the valley." We made a stalk down through the muskeg and, sure enough, at about 75 yards there stood a nice mountain silver tip looking at us. After a fine shot, we skinned him out and got back to camp in time for supper. My pals thought I was very lucky!

One morning Craig, my guide, and I were riding along a creek bottom when we spotted a nice bull caribou at about 300 yards up a 45-degree angle. I slid off my horse, sat down on the trail and fired. Three things happened; I got a fine half moon scope cut over my right eye, the horse took off and the bull went down! I wiped the blood out of my eye...Craig went after my horse and then we made the climb. Naturally he beat me by 50 yards. The caribou was a mature bull and he now looks great on my trophy room wall. Later I looked at my rifle, a Model 70 .300 Mag. The bang to my eye had cracked the scope lens so I had to shoot my moose with a 270 Win. Lesson: Always bring two rifles!

Another day we had made a climb on foot only to come back to find my horse gone. Apparently I hadn't tied her lead rope well enough. She had a colt in the corral back at camp and like all good mothers wanted to be with her baby. Craig and I took turns riding and walking the five miles back to camp.

Fishing is always good in the northern lakes and this one was no exception. We had trout and grayling on Mepps spinners whenever we wished.

The other two fellows in camp were an interesting pair. One was a doctor from Cologne, Germany, and the other a dentist from Ogden, Utah. During the Second World War the German was a Messerschmitt pilot and was shot down over the North Atlantic. Americans rescued him and sent him to a POW camp in California. He had had one year of medical school in Germany so he was sent to be an assistant to the man in charge of the dental office, our friend from Utah. They became good friends and hunted together many times.

On the last day of the hunt, I made a stalk on some caribou with one of my pals. He shot a nice bull on top of the hill and Leon, the other guide, thought it would be closer for him to take the horns down the other side on foot and we should go back the other way and get the horses. He told us his horse would find the

Four happy Yukon hunters: Don, Jim, Maury and Pete.

trail. What a joke!

At sundown we were at a complete loss as to where the trail was. Finally my pal's horse sensed the right trail and we were on our way out and back to camp. When we finally got in Gordy had a lantern lit and was on his horse coming out to look for us.

At about 10 a.m. we heard the familiar drone of a Beaver plane and soon were heading back to Watson Lake and the three days back down the AlCan Highway. My suburban had four sleeping bags, four caribou racks and three moose racks on top. Inside there were four duffel bags, eight rifles, two bear hides, a sheep cape, a goat cape and four tired, dirty but very happy hunters.

I would, again, like to quote Robert Service:

There's a land-oh, it beckons and beckons,
I want to go back—I will.

When you exit the plane at the Anchorage International Airport, the first thing you'll notice is the clean, cool, fresh air. The second is the full body mounts of native Alaskan wildlife. The third thing you'll notice are all the bear attack books at the airport bookstores! Just opening one of those books and reading some paragraphs can send numbing chills up a person's spine. I mumbled to myself, "Glad it's them and not me."

'Bous, Bears and Books in Alaska

by NAHC Member Bert Westover
of Spokane, Washington

My second hunting trip to Alaska was hopefully going to be more relaxed, more successful and much more fun than my first. Not that my first hunt in Alaska wasn't relaxed, successful or fun—it was actually all three—after all, I did take a fine bull moose and caribou. The quarry this time out was the same as on my first safari in Alaska—moose and caribou.

By the time I returned to the airport to pick up my hunting partner, Jon, I had already taken a big bull caribou. I had spotted it from about two miles away, where I stood atop an old water tower that had been part of a turn-of-the-century cannery. The wood on the tower was old and dry-rotted, and I had to examine every step for strength. In southern Alaska where the land is flat and rolling, a vantage point like this was necessary for long-distance glassing. From this tower I could see close to two dozen caribou, maybe half of them bulls. After glassing for about 30 minutes and field judging the size of the bulls, I began my nearly two-hour stalk. (It hadn't helped that the caribou kept changing locations.) When I was about 200 yards from them, I got down on my belly and crawled. At about 100 yards, a lagging bull spotted my movement. As the herd turned to see what the fuss was all about, I aimed my crosshairs on the chest of the lead bull and fired. That shot went in the front shoulder but was not fatal. Standing up, I chambered another round and took aim. The hollow thud of the second shot and the caribou dropping hard indicated that my .30-06 rifle and I had done our jobs. Waiting for Jon, I was pretty well pumped and primed on getting our tags filled with a giant bull moose and caribou.

When Jon came through the terminal, I told him what a great hunter I was—I meant what a great hunt I had. Our ride to the campsite was on a fishing vessel we christened "The Alaskan Queen," a diesel-burning, oil-smelling, barely together, barely running nightmare. Now, we all have seen different shades of green, but I believe I discovered a new one when I looked at Jon's face an hour into the cruise. Jon was very seasick.

Arriving at what was to be our home for the next two weeks, I unpacked our supplies and made camp while Jon sat on shore

---

Polar Bear Import Permits Available

Hunters may apply for permits to bring into the United States legally taken polar bear trophies from specific Canadian populations.

The money earned from permit fees is earmarked for polar bear conservation, specifically to develop and implement cooperative research and management programs to conserve polar bears in Alaska and Russia. This is good news for hunters and good news for bears.

For more information, visit http://www.fws.gov/@sbh:r9dia/polarbfs.html.

Source: U.S. Fish & Wildlife Service

struggling to find his true skin color. Once camp was set, we turned our work efforts into preparing a fire and cooking up some food. The five gallon bucket I turned upside-down to use as a seat had been there from another camp. I could not understand why anybody would puncture holes in a good bucket, and we discussed over a bowl of chili what kind of nut would do such a thing. When Jon put his fingers in the holes, it became clear what kind of nut had made them: a bear—a big, man-eating bear—just like the ones in those airport books.

That first night in the tent, both of us held loaded and ready guns. I doubt that either of us would have been much help to the other because if that bear had started on Jon first, I had planned a gunny sack race down the trail in my sleeping bag as fast as my legs could bounce. I would hope that any shots I might have fired in my last courageous moments in the tent would find their mark on the bear (or at least put Jon out of a miserably agonizing death).

But we made it through the night to find the next day greeting us with a rain shower. (That's pretty much par for the course in Alaska.) Both of use were quite anxious to start hunting despite our obvious lack of sleep. Just 20 minutes into our hunt, we spotted a cow moose. Another 20 minutes later, Jon was following me across his first muskeg. As I crossed to the other side in a few easy-looking strides, Jon followed my lead but suddenly began taking another route. Walking across muskeg takes skill, and once you learn this skill, it's a piece of cake, but until then it's trial and error. So Jon found out through error how deep and cold a muskeg's water is and how hip waders full of muskeg water feel. But Jon's a good sport, and by golly, this was not going to ruin his hunt. So we took off to find our record book bulls.

After hours of hiking and glassing, we concluded on our way back to camp that the day's best sign of bulls or any animals was the few caribou sheds we had found. It was not the sign we had hoped for, but four or five nice 'bou sheds have got to mean something good. Our hopes were still high when about 100 yards from camp—while walking a trail and not paying attention to what was going on around us—we darn near walked up on and straddled a big bull moose. He was as surprised to see us as we were to see him! We had about two seconds to figure out whether he was legal or not—he wasn't. The sheds and that big bull made good conversation over dinner.

That night at dinner we sure were wishing for some fresh meat to eat with all the vegetables we had brought. Fajitas, stir-frys and other camp foods were becoming less appetizing without the meat—and I had shipped my caribou back home for storage. We turned our need for record book bulls into the need for frying pan vittles!

The next few days just kept giving us opportunities to see all the same things over and over again. Jon was convinced the only reason we were finding so many sheds was that the herds would come to this area and run through it as quickly as possible to get to greener pastures, tripping and knocking a horn off in the process!

The day came for us to do some real hiking. We planned to travel down river five or six miles to get our meat. At about noon, we spotted a small herd of caribou. This was it, all or bust. An hour later when we got to the herd, it turned out to be just an old cow and her calf. But looking around we found another herd and went on our way to investigate. This herd turned out to be three small bulls and one old cow. As we grew desperate for shootable game, we had decided to try some caribou luring techniques. The first was calling; with our deep moans through cupped hands, the caribou must have thought we were helpless animals in pain. They weren't concerned. The second trick was to put sheds on top our heads and slowly make our way to them. That worked about as well as a soup sandwich; the caribou made tracks quickly! As we decided to head back toward camp, the group of bulls had made their way into a dried-up, sandy lake bed 100 yards away. This was it. We would shoot one of these bulls for camp meat and end our newly acquired vegetarian eating habits.

Jon shot his first caribou that day, and though it was no wall hanger, its meat was a welcome treat that night for dinner. When we returned to the kill site the next morning, the carcass didn't quite look the same as we had left it. There was no animal or gut

Photo by Norm Kerr

pile! The hair started standing up on my back, and I wanted to find my way back to camp as soon as possible. Jon just wanted to find his animal.

It took us about five minutes to figure out what took Jon's 'bou. A big bear—that man-eating bear—was our guess. We took a few pictures and boogied on out of there, looking behind us with every other step.

As we turned in that night, it didn't seem to bother Jon that there might be a bear looking to eat some fine, pink flesh, just like the kind we had. While he was fast asleep in his sleeping bag, I was starting to notice how our tent looked like a giant stay-fresh, zip-lock baggie! At any minute, I expected to see a bear's paw quietly unzipping the fly and tossing in some seasoning! When I awoke the next morning, I realized how great it felt to be alive.

That evening right after dinner we could hear someone screaming profanities from a boat. Not able to make out full sentences, we weren't concerned—until we began to make out my name being yelled with those profanities! Jon hadn't quite gotten to the frightened stage yet, so while I was panicking, he deciphered the words, "Bert, break your @#*%*~ camp now!" It was Chad, and he obviously wanted us to break camp and quick! Later we learned that a big storm had been heading our way.

By the time Chad got his boat to our shore, we were ready. After loading our gear on board, we all discussed our successes and our failures on this hunting trip. None of us wanted to be the one to say that in a sad way, we were glad to be heading home. The boat ride was the beginning of the end of our Alaskan adventure. After cleaning The Alaskan Queen, we were all flight-bound for home. Leaving Anchorage is a bit of a sad experience. No place that I know of in the Lower 48 has the beauty Alaska has to offer. So until my next Alaskan safari, I'll have all these great pictures and memories to recall for pleasure…along with a book I bought at the airport to read for suspense.

Longer Licenses

To make your hunting license last longer, coat it with laminate after you sign it. For less than $5 at most discount stores, you can buy a sheet of laminate to coat both sides. Wet weather won't affect your license if you cover it with this clear plastic.

The black bears in northern Alberta have been known to raise many a hunter's pulse rates on several occasions. My sons had their pulses raised by bears up there on our family hunting trip. This hunt was 17-year-old Jeremy's and 16-year-old Chris' second expe-riences with hunt-ing black bear around baited sites. Both boys were fortunate in tagging six-foot sows, their first bears with a bow, the previous year. And although their first adven-

Big Bruins of the Northcountry Brush

by NAHC Member Kathy Butt of Portland, Tennessee

ture gave them a pretty good idea of what they could expect while hunting bears around baited sites, they were quite unprepared for their meetings with those big bad Alberta bruins.

My husband, Foster, and I have made it a point to include our two sons each year on a family hunting adventure. When Foster and I flew into McNalley Lake in northeastern Alberta, Canada, a few years ago, we knew immediately that this was one adven-ture we wanted to share with our sons. Jeremy and Chris weren't inexperienced at hunting big game since they've hunted for whitetail and elk with archery equipment, blackpowder firearms and rifles. But without a doubt, it was this spring black bear hunt that will be the adventure both will fondly reminisce about for years to come.

Jeremy and his guide, Dave Archer, headed out to hunt the Trapper's Bridge bait site on the first evening's hunt. The adventure began when Jeremy arrowed a nice seven-foot black bear. Trailing the bear turned out to be a hair-raising experience for both Jeremy and Dave. Thick jack pines and fallen timber made trailing a little hairy and as the two approached the bear they could still hear him breathing. Dave instructed Jeremy to nock another arrow and to be ready to shoot, should it be necessary.

Suddenly, the bear stood upright and Jeremy reacted by taking a step backward and stumbling over a fallen log. Luckily Dave was right behind him to prevent his falling while the bear ran only a few short yards before going down within eyesight. This time, Jeremy was more prepared and slipped quietly to within 15 yards of the bruin and placed another arrow into both lungs. The bear was down and Jeremy had his seven-footer.

Meanwhile, Chris and Foster traveled to a bait site the guides had nicknamed "Cannibal Ridge," a site located several miles up the river. During the four weeks prior to Chris's scheduled hunt, several hunters had hunted the site but had never seen the big bear that had been covering up the bait site. Large tracks, enormous piles of scat and the continuance of the bait site being covered up by the ghostly bruin no one had yet seen had some hunters spooked.

There was no doubt, this was a big bear. Foster and Chris decided it was well worth the time it might take to wait it out. It was on the third evening's hunt that the two met up with the bruin they'd been hunting for.

Chris and Foster were stationed in their treestands 15 yards from the bait site and had been there for almost two hours before two young bears romped in and scavenged pastries and meat scraps from the bait pile. Foster was in a stand to Chris's right with a video camera and taping the hunt. The cubs played around for almost an hour before a big bear sent the cubs scurrying up a tree. That's when Chris and his dad spotted the approaching bruin. There was no doubt that this was a Pope & Young contender. This bear would easily square more than seven foot. The enormous black beast slowly waddled to the bait site and gave the two hunters a good opportunity to look him over.

When the bear picked up a frozen piece of meat and sauntered off out of range for the second time, Foster discovered Chris was suffering a little freeze panic. After a little coaching and reassurance from his dad, Chris was ready when the bear approached the bait site for the third time. Chris's problem was getting his bow drawn. This was a really big bear,

Jeremy Butt of Portland, Tennessee, proudly displays the bruin he arrowed while hunting in Alberta's north country.

and Chris was definitely more than a little shook up.

Chris's dad was getting worried at this point and as the bear turned to leave the site once again, Foster tried to sound like an annoying squirrel to make the bear stop and turn around. At 20 yards out, the bear stopped and turned, offering Chris a broadside shot. "Chris, there's your shot, but you've got to shoot now. Take a deep breath and calm down; you don't have much time. The bear's not going to stick around," Foster pleaded.

The bear was looking right at Chris as he finally managed to come to full draw. Foster noticed the arrow shaking and knew Chris was struggling to maintain his composure. The squirrel noises had piqued the bear's curiosity and held its attention while

Chris sighted in on the spot behind the bruin's front shoulder. He released the string and watched as the arrow slammed into the bear's midsection, a little farther back than he would have liked. The black bruin whirled and roared out of sight. Chris thought his heart was going to jump out of his chest.

Both Foster and Chris were somewhat worried about Chris's shot placement and decided retrieving the bear was going to have to wait until morning. They wanted to give the bear plenty of time to expire. The time was 10:00 in the evening and they only had an hour of daylight left. They thought it would be best to head back to camp and return the following morning to track Chris's big bear. They spent a restless night in camp.

Guide Harvey McNally, Foster and Chris all returned the next morning to track the bear. Harvey and Foster were armed with rifles while Chris carried his bow. The area was thick with jack pines, fallen timber and ferns. Foster and Harvey both knew tracking a wounded bear through this stuff could be potentially dangerous, but were hoping Chris's bear was down for the count.

A healthy blood trail led the three for more than 300 yards when all hell broke loose. A big black bear jumped up and exploded from the area in front of the hunters. Assuming it was Chris' bear, Foster shouldered his rifle and was able to connect on the bear at 80 yards. The bear whirled and ran straight back at the three hunters, with Harvey firing another shot into the approaching bear. The three heard the bear go down almost at the location where they'd first jumped it up. Foster and Harvey felt bad for Chris. Chris was also feeling pretty down and out at their having to put his trophy down with firearms.

That feeling of despair quickly turned into amazement when they discovered the big bear the riflemen had just shot wasn't Chris's bear but an even bigger bear that had been feeding on Chris's bear. Talk about excitement! Lying on the ground were two big bears. Chris's bear had gone down through the night and had been covered completely in ferns by the bigger bear. The bear that they'd just shot had returned to feed on Chris's bear. Turns out, Chris's bear, squaring seven feet two inches, wasn't the crit-

Chris Butt of Portland, Tennessee, with the black bear he arrowed in Alberta while hunting with his mom and dad.

ter responsible for covering the bait site. The big bad bruin of Cannibal Ridge was the bigger seven feet five inch bear Foster finished off. Foster placed his bear tag on the bigger bruin.

This is one hunting adventure the entire family will be talking about for years to come. Hunters can—and quite often do—experience the unusual when hunting those aggressive Alberta bears. Just ask Jeremy and Chris. They'll be quick to tell you just how exciting it really can be!

Bear Steak

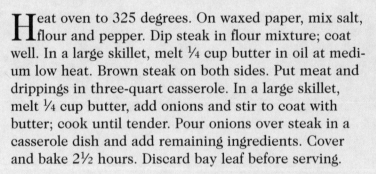

⅓ cup flour
1 tsp. salt
1 tsp. pepper
2 lbs. bear round-
    steak, 1 inch thick
½ cup butter, divided
2 tbsp. olive oil
4 medium onions, thinly sliced
1½ cups beer
¼ tsp. dried marjoram leaves
¼ tsp. dried thyme leaves
1 bay leaf

Heat oven to 325 degrees. On waxed paper, mix salt, flour and pepper. Dip steak in flour mixture; coat well. In a large skillet, melt ¼ cup butter in oil at medium low heat. Brown steak on both sides. Put meat and drippings in three-quart casserole. In a large skillet, melt ¼ cup butter, add onions and stir to coat with butter; cook until tender. Pour onions over steak in a casserole dish and add remaining ingredients. Cover and bake 2½ hours. Discard bay leaf before serving.

NAHC Member Mike Hinton
McKinleyville, OH

My departure day found me heading north to Zealand, New Brunswick, to hunt with NAHC Approved Guide and Outfitter Malarkey's Cabin Guiding Service. I arrived in bear hunting camp to meet other hunters and my guide, Ray Dillon. Some of the hunters in camp were bow-hunters, and I watched them practice with their equipment in preparation for their hunt. We had many things to talk about as we shared plentiful meals and the luxuries of the camp over the next week.

The Base Bear

by NAHC Member Armand Gagnon
of Manchester, New Hampshire

I was excited as I headed to my stand that first evening. I was also surprised to discover that I would be sitting in a lawn chair about 30 yards from the bait! I built a hasty blind of brush around me and settled in. There was not much action to report those first evenings but a pattern quickly developed. The rifle hunters would not see any bears, but the archery hunters would come back to camp with tales of seeing numerous bears. At least someone was seeing bears. A few evenings later, I returned to camp to see a bear swinging from the meat pole. I discovered the bowhunter's practice had brought results. Now every hunter in camp had higher spirits.

We were hunting on a military base in Canada that required special permits for access, and Ray was one of the few outfitters with permission. On the next to last day of the hunt, Ray informed the other gun hunters and me that a camp of soldiers on a military maneuver was having trouble with a bear. The commandant had asked Ray to provide a hunter to take the bear. We three rifle hunters threw our names in a hat, and my luck turned for the better when my name was drawn as the lucky hunter.

Ray drove me to the military bivouac camp in the woods, and we were quickly surrounded by soldiers. There were more than 400 soldiers in the area with tents, trucks and lots of military equipment parked around. The soldiers wanted to see my rifle and hunting gear and asked many questions. I learned that a big black bear had been raiding their camp and had stolen more than 20 loaves of bread and torn several tents. The problem bear had also been entering tents and stealing food from the soldiers.

Ray finally had to ask the troops that followed us into the woods to leave so I could hunt. I set up a hunting blind location behind their camp at the edge of a clearing. Ray set a bait nearby and placed molasses over a Sterno burner; the sweet smell would attract any bear passing through the area. I knew I had to make a clean one-shot kill for the safety of the soldiers and to help Ray stay on good terms with the base officials. Much pressure was riding on my shoulders as I sat and waited for the bear to appear. Ray stayed there with me to help watch for bears.

Suddenly, Ray whispered that he saw a huge bear approaching us. Spotting the bear, I raised my rifle and found its shoulder in my scope. When I shot, the bear flinched and ran away. I could see blood running down its side and knew I had made a good hit.

When I started to look for the bear, I heard a commotion behind me and looked to see more than 75 curious soldiers streaming from camp and toward me. The last thing I wanted was a mob in the woods with a possibly wounded bear running around in the brush. Fortunately, Ray got the situation under control and turned the troops back to camp.

We tracked the bear a short distance into the brush and found

NAHC Member Armand Gagnon with his black bear from the base.

it lying dead. When we knew all was safe, Ray hollered for the troops to come and see the bear. We were instantly surrounded by 75 soldiers who wanted to take a close look at the bear. Many of them wanted to feel the bear's fur, paws, teeth and head. Ray and I just stepped aside and let them swirl around the bear. I answered hundreds of questions before we got the bear field dressed. I discovered my shot had gone through its lungs and completely demolished the bear's heart. The huge bruin had an estimated live weight of nearly 300 pounds.

We loaded the bear up with the help of the soldiers and headed back to camp. The next day, I left camp and headed for home with fond memories of an exciting hunt at the military base. My bear rug brings back the memories every time I look at it.

NORTH AMERICAN HUNTING CLUB

T I P

HUNTING CAMP LORE

Checklist to Take a Super Slam

If you like to hunt, then you'll want to set your sights on a Super Slam. To achieve this, you'll need to take a:

Columbia blacktail deer	Alaska brown bear
Black bear	Mountain lion
Mule deer	Roosevelt elk
Canada moose	Quebec-Labrador caribou
White-tailed deer	Polar bear
Pronghorn	Coues' deer
Alaska-Yukon moose	Woodland caribou
Rocky Mountain goat	Shiras moose
Yellowstone elk	Muskox
Barren ground caribou	Desert sheep
Sitka black-tailed deer	Bison
Dall sheep	Bighorn sheep
Mountain caribou	Stone sheep

My story begins in the spring of 1994, when I was working for the Forest Service as a wildland firefighter. A good friend called one evening to tell me that he had harvested a nice black bear—his second one. "I left my baits set up for you," Mark said. "Why don't you come out on your days off and do some hunting?" He suggested that I bring my muzzleloader and my mountain bike. He said one of the baits was up a big canyon and the bike would make a quicker trip to check it.

Blackpowder Bear

by NAHC Charter Member
Keith Gould of Upton, Wyoming

From my home, it is a six-hour drive to Mark's, then another hour and a half to the hunt area. I left after work and drove to Mark's home. We got up the next day and went to check the baits. The first bait was at the end of the bike trip up this long canyon. The countryside was a sight to see in early June. Everything was green and plush and spring was in full swing.

We checked four baits that day. I had never hunted bear before, so I was asking a lot of questions. Since Mark has hunted bears for a long time, he gave me enough information to keep me out of trouble. After checking all the baits, he thought my best bet would be the bait in "Bear Draw." Over several years, this location produced four bears for Mark and his friends. Mark had to work swing shift that day, so he left me by myself, and said I should be at the bait about 4:00p.m.

After about a half hour, I was getting bored, so I went to the location early. After putting fresh bait in the barrel, I set up about 90 yards across a little meadow and proceeded to wait. After a long drive the night before and the long bike ride that morning, coupled with the warm afternoon sun, I soon fell asleep. About an hour later, I was awakened by a noise that sounded like a pickup door being closed. My truck was only a quarter of a mile away on the county road. I thought someone was messing with it, and I almost went to investigate, but then I heard the noise again. This time it came from behind the bait.

I looked through my binoculars and saw a bear in the trees on the hill past the bait. As I watched the bear, it came to the bait and didn't stop. It went to my trail in the grass where I had walked across the meadow and started trailing me.

There I was, laying on my back, looking through 10X binoculars at a bear sniffing my trail at less than 100 yards. Did I mention my .54 caliber Hawkens was leaning against a tree at my feet? Since I was a novice at bear hunting, I had my Ruger Redhawk pistol for backup. I grabbed that, pulled back the hammer and waited for the bear to get within ten yards or so. The bear stopped at 30 yards, sniffed the air, woofed a couple of times then went back to the bait. Needless to say, I was quite relieved!

While the bear headed back, I sat up, took my rifle, slid it over a tree limb and waited for the bear to put its head in the bait barrel. When the time was right, I took careful aim and...I couldn't see my black front sight on the black bear! I moved over to the sun on the grass and re-centered my front sight in the tang-mounted peep and moved it onto the bear. I realized that bears have no definition; they are just a big black ball of fur at that distance. I centered on what I figured to be a quartering away shot just behind the right shoulder. I slowly pulled back the hammer, pulled the set trigger, let out a breath and dropped the hammer.

The gun went off, a cloud of smoke drifted out across the meadow and all hell broke loose!

The bear charged up the hill in the direction it had come from into the thick lodgepole pines. After calming myself down, I reloaded and went to check for a blood trail. There was none. I followed the narrow trail the bear had taken all the way to the top of the ridge. I could feel the veins in my neck pound with every beat of my heart. I could hear even the slightest sound. The ground was hard, so I could not see any tracks to speak of. The other side of the ridge was semi-open and I glassed the area. I saw no sign of the bear.

I had planned to go back and check for blood with the tried and proven method of using toilet paper. I was just about to break out of the trees by the bait when I looked off to my right. Not 20 yards off the trail was this black ball of fur! After throwing sticks and rocks for a couple of minutes, I figured it was safe enough to take a closer look. I set down my rifle and pulled my Redhawk. I inched my way closer, reached out my foot and gave the bear a couple of kicks. DEAD BEAR! I realized then how lucky I was that the bear was dead. I had passed by it not ten minutes earlier and didn't see it.

The bear was an average-sized dry sow. After field dressing and getting her loaded in the truck, which was quite a chore, I headed for town. When I arrived, I was surrounded by police. No, I wasn't in trouble. Mark is an officer, and news travels fast in a small Wyoming town. The game biologist who checked my bear, which is a requirement in Wyoming, estimated its weight at 250 pounds. The hide squared 5½ feet. I received a card from the University of Wyoming stating the tests done on the teeth showed the bear to be 6½ years old. I was back in town at 7:30 p.m., making my first bear hunt last a total of about eight hours in the field. I was lucky. I have a good friend who knows bears. I learned a lot from Mark and the experience of that hunt.

After skinning the bear, we found that the bullet entered the left hindquarter, traveled the full length of the body at an angle and stopped short of going through the hide on the right shoulder. The pelvic bone was broken as was the right shoulder blade. The bullet retained all of its weight and was flattened on the front and down one side.

Bears are tough animals. After being shot with a heavy bullet that took out its vitals and broke major bones, the bear still ran uphill through thick timber a good 75 yards!

I will never forget my first bear hunt. Thanks, Mark!

Drive Defensively in Moose Country

Moose are a threat to motorists, but there are precautions you can take to help avoid hitting them, according to the Vermont Fish & Wildlife Department. Moose will appear along the road-side to lick salt in the gravel.

Here are some precautions to keep in mind when driving in moose country:

- Always be aware of the danger—moose cross the road randomly, as well as their regular crossings.

- Increase your roadside awareness when you see "Moose" signs along the highway.

- Drive defensively and don't overdrive your headlights.

- If you see a moose ahead, slow down or stop. Trying to speed past them "before they can move" can be a serious mistake.

*C*aribou is such a wonderful-sounding word. Just the mere mention of "caribou" evokes scenes of herds of white, gray and brown, regal, majestic, antler-bedecked animals moving slowly across a barren tundra. Their land is harsh and unforgiving, but it's also one of great beauty with its muted colors of greens, browns and reds royally studded with caribou bulls in the fall, their magnificent antlers still in velvet or polished for

Caribou at Long Last

by Larry Weishuhn,
North American Hunter
"Whitetails" Columnist

the fall moon of madness. How I used to long to visit the land of the caribou! And now I cannot wait to go back.

As a youngster growing up in rural Texas, thousands of miles from the nearest caribou, I dreamed of hunting the great deer of the North Country. I read everything I could find about caribou and talked to friends of my dad who had made the journey north (in our little rural ranching community, there were not many who even knew what a caribou was, much less had hunted them), and I continued to learn more about caribou, dreaming of the day I would finally hunt the majestic animals!

I saw my first caribou in 1977 as one of four U.S.-

based wildlife biologists to participate in an international snow goose banding venture in the northern reaches of Canada's Northwest Territories. During the six weeks I spent just below the Arctic Circle, I saw thousands of caribou on their annual migration. It was a scene I will never forget. There were little bulls, big bulls and then "aaahh" bulls with unbelievably huge antlers. Seeing them only deepened my resolve to one day hunt them.

It was not until the early fall of 1996 that I was able to venture north for caribou, primarily as a guest of Tourisme Quebec and Jack Hume Adventures, on a hunt arranged for me through Siegfried Gagnon. The idea for the hunt was initiated that spring during NAHC's Jamboree in Nashville, Tennessee. There, I met fellow NAHC member Denver McCormick. After visiting briefly, Denver and I realized our interests were so close to the same it was scary. Talking with him was like talking to a long-lost old friend. Right then and there we resolved to hunt caribou that fall. And we did!

While caribou are without a doubt the most beautiful of the deer clan, they can also be the most unpredictable. Our hunt took us about 200 miles north of Schefferville, Quebec, to a legendary camp that caribou had always passed on their previous annual migrations. Landing in front of camp in a float plane made the caribou hunt, which until then had simply seemed like a dream, feel like reality.

We quickly stowed our gear in our comfortable cabin, checked our rifles to be sure they were still shooting where they were supposed to and, as fast as we could, gathered our hunting gear. Alfred, our campmaster, took us across the long, narrow lake to spend the afternoon hunting caribou.

That first afternoon, Denver and I watched several small groups of caribou cows, calves and yearling bulls. We did see one big bull, but he was about two miles away, and we saw him just before it was time to head back to the lake to be picked up for the night.

The next morning, we were up early and again headed across

Larry Weishuhn with his hard-earned caribou.

the lake to spend the day glassing the barrens where previously caribou herds had traveled. Their trails in the fragile tundra were as obvious as highways on the prairie. For thousands of years, caribou had passed through the area. We hunted hard, then about mid-afternoon Denver and I split up. He was to watch several trails not far from the lake's shore while I watched the barrens.

Later that afternoon I heard two shots. I watched and waited, and when nothing showed, I made my way to where my hunting partner had taken up his vigil.

From a distance, I could see Denver, obviously looking at something on the ground. Then I could see it was a nice caribou bull. I ran to where he stood and quickly congratulated him on his first caribou bull. Seeing four bulls, Denver had immediately picked out the best of the group and shot. Then he picked out the second biggest bull and had taken him as well. I was excited for Denver. He had done well!

During the next several days, I hunted hard from daylight until dark, but each day, the number of caribou I saw decreased. On the last two days of our hunt, I saw nary a caribou. Such is caribou hunting—quite often it is either feast or famine. Although I did not take a bull on that hunt, the hunting experience was one of my best ever. I had a blast and hunted hard, often in adverse weather. It was great! Before leaving northern Quebec, I promised to return to the land of the caribou as soon as possible!

"Their trails in the fragile tundra were as obvious as highways on the prairie."

Back home, I made arrangements to again hunt with Jack Hume the following fall. With another quick call, Denver had agreed to go back with me.

Thankfully, there were other hunts to occupy my year—whitetails, mule deer, elk and, during the spring, black bear. Finally, it was time to again head north to the land of the caribou.

From Montreal we flew to Schefferville, and as soon as we landed, the fog rolled in. For the next three days, we sat on the ground and kept waiting for the word to fly to camp. Jack Hume's comfortable base camp in Schefferville and members of our hunting party made the wait bearable.

After an eternity and several mooseburgers too many, we—Denver and me, a couple from Pennsylvania and two brothers from Maine—reached camp. To say we were anxious to hunt would have been an understatement!

Under the guidance of Tom, our campmaster, we hunted

hard for several days and saw young bulls and a few cows but no sizable bulls. It was beginning to look like a repeat performance of the previous September. Then the campmaster gave the word: "Get ready. You're moving to another camp this afternoon." It took some effort to round up the troops, but we finally got it done.

Later that afternoon, I sat on a river crossing. Almost immediately, a sizable bull came walking up along the bank and then lay down about 400 yards from where I was hidden. I could see his antler tops and part of his main beams. Both appeared to be pretty good, but I wanted to see what else would come by.

During the next hour, several small herds of young bulls and cows walked within less than 50 yards of my hiding place behind a big rock. Finally, I again looked at the bedded bull and then noticed movement heading its way. Eight bulls, including one that looked pretty good, walked within sight. As they walked by the bedded bull, it stood up. Only then did I realize how big it was! Both in body and antler it dwarfed the other bulls.

Immediately, I got my rifle chambered for .30-06 in shooting position. When the bull closed the distance to about 300 yards, I squeezed the trigger and down it went. I shot the bull a second time and then started working my way toward it, which required walking around a small lake.

At its side, I could not believe the bull's size. It was huge. Although in years past, its antlers had likely been better, the antlers still had a wide spread, extremely long main beams and small double shovels. I was ecstatic! My lifelong dream had finally come true; even after 50 years, it had been worth the wait. Others in our camp did equally well that day. Such is caribou hunting in the land of the barrens.

Caribou hunting is, in my opinion, thoroughly enjoyable; however, like other hunting, at times it can be strenuous, heartbreaking, disappointing, joyous and downright fun! To me, bull caribou antlers are the most beautiful of all the deer species. Like all deer species, each rack is different from the next. Compared to other big game hunts, hunting caribou, especially in Quebec, is relatively inexpensive, and the chances of success are considerably better than hunting elk. On top of everything, caribou meat is excellent. Quite frankly, I can't get enough of caribou hunting! Theirs is a land to which I want return again and again and again…

Venison Pepper Steak

6 tbsp. butter or margarine, divided
½ cup onion, chopped
¾ cup beef broth
2 tbsp. red wine
¼ tsp. sugar
1 tbsp. fresh ground
    pepper
¼ cup Brandy
4-6 venison steaks, 1-inch thick

Melt 3 tbs. butter on medium heat in medium sized skillet. Add onion; stir until golden. Add broth, wine and sugar. Cook and reduce by half. Coat steaks with pepper on both sides. Melt 3 tbsp. butter on medium heat. When steaks are done, place them on a heated platter. Remove skillet from heat, add brandy, heat over low heat, remove from burner, ignite, wait until flames die. Add onion mix to brandy, bring to boil while stirring, pour sauce over steaks, serve!

Vernon A. Denzer
Dane, WI

*H*unting with a muzzleloader is one of the fastest growing shooting sports in the country today. At the turn of the century there were approximately 500,000 white-tailed deer nationwide. Now, as a result of conservation efforts from the state wildlife agencies and sportsmen, our whitetail population has exploded to more than 20 million!

Muzzleloading is becoming an important game management tool used by almost

Muzzleloading Success

by NAHC Member Rick O'Shea
of Centerville, Iowa

every state and province in North America. The chance to go afield with a muzzleloading rifle provides hunters the opportunity to hunt in less crowded conditions in early seasons prior to general rifle or shotgun seasons. In many cases, the hunter can harvest additional deer by accepting the limitations of a muzzleloader.

It's a fact that today's hunter is becoming a three-season hunter: archery, rifle or shotgun, and muzzleloader. When a hunter elects to use a muzzleloading rifle, there are certain tips and techniques that will make muzzleloader hunting more enjoyable. Here are a few that I've picked up over the years.

Always snap caps. Make sure the rifle is unloaded and pointed in a safe direction. When you get ready to load, snap a couple of caps to clear oil and grease from the bore and nipple. I used to point the muzzle of my rifle at the ground and snap a couple of caps and look for the dirt or grass to move. Well, I've found a surefire way to know that I'm getting a clean burn. Dampen a patch with saliva and run it down the bore until it rests on top of the breech plug. Snap two or three caps and remove the patch. You'll notice a dark burn spot that the caps made on the bottom of the patch. This is how you know the fire is getting through the nipple to the breech area. Also, the patch will absorb oil or grease left in the bore from a previous cleaning.

Use fresh powder. Always start your season with a fresh can of powder. This is one way you can really increase your performance! There's nothing worse than finding out that the powder you thought was in mint condition was contaminated with moisture and caused a hangfire or even a misfire. There are a variety of powders available for the muzzleloading hunter: Black Powder FFG, Pyrodex RS, Select and, my favorite, pellets. If you use the pellets, be sure that you allow ample time for the barrel to cool between shots. This is very important if you're sighting your rifle in the warm days of late summer. I found that as the barrel heats up, the accuracy out of my rifle will decrease with every shot. For better performance, take your time when reloading at the bench, and you should see groups to brag about.

Bullet selection is everything. It's important to tailor the powder charge and the bullet with the type of game that you're hunting. I've talked to a number of hunters who constantly complain about "expensive muzzleloading bullets." In fact, I used to be one of them. Then, I really thought about it. The bullet is the most critical component of a muzzleloader. A single bullet will either make or break a hunt. I've learned through experience that this is one area to avoid cutting corners.

There are three types of ammunition you can use in a muzzleloading rifle: round balls, heavy lead conicals and sabot bullets. I've had the best success using a 250- or 260-grain bullet with a black sabot with 100 grains of powder. This is my standard load for white-tailed deer. If you're hunting a variety of game, here are some sample loads that have worked well for me.

Game Bullet Weight Powder

Animal	Bullet	Powder
Pronghorn & Mule Deer	220-, 250- & 260-grain sabot	100 Grains FFG
White-tailed deer	220-, 250- & 260-grain sabot	100 Grains FFG
Elk, Caribou, Moose or Bear	250-, 260-, 300- & 325-grain sabot	110 Grains FFG

Swab between shots. Another way to improve the accuracy and performance of your muzzleloader is to swab inside the barrel between shots, especially at the bench. I dampen a patch with a little bit of saliva and run it down the bore with short strokes. Never take one long stroke down the bore or the patch will get stuck. This happens if the patch isn't damp enough. If you've got a muzzleloader with a breech plug, just take the rifle apart and push the patch out the receiver. Swabbing is critical to performance. Since muzzleloading is a "dirty" sport you want to keep the muzzleloader as clean as possible. Too much residue inside the bore will cause your rifle to be difficult to load and your accuracy to decrease. However, when I'm afield and I've taken my shot, I don't recommend taking the time to swab unless you know the game is down for good. Otherwise, stick to the "three R's" when you're in the woods…reload, reload, reload!

Stuck patch syndrome. Here's a neat little trick I learned recently for "stuck patch syndrome." If you are swabbing between shots and the patch does get stuck, pour a little bit of water down the bore to help moisten the patch. Work the ramrod back and forth to loosen the patch, and it should come right out. Sometimes dry patches get stuck and need a little help. Finally, take a dampened patch to clean the residue and dry out the bore.

Muzzleloading opens up new seasons and challenges to big game hunters.

Oil and muzzleloaders do mix. For a long time hunters have been afraid to really oil their muzzleloader. Blackpowder is really corrosive because of the sulfur content. Clean your rifle with solvent or water and make sure that it is oiled heavily, especially if it is going to be stored until next season. I think the phobia about oil comes from hunters who had previous experiences with traditional muzzleloaders. If you don't snap caps and swab the bore before you initially load your rifle, the powder charge will get contaminated with excess oil and you will have hangfires and misfires.

Know where your accessories are located. It is important to know where your loading accessories are located when you head to the woods. I personally have consolidated my accessories to eliminate the possibles bag. I've found that when I'm in a hurry to reload I can now find what I need in a timely manner. Here's how I organize my accessories for every muzzleloading hunt. I place a few patches and a cleaning jag in my left pants pocket, three speed loaders in my right pants pocket and a capper in my left shirt pocket. This is all you need to make your muzzleloader work afield, and it's organized for a fast second shot.

Practice, Practice and Practice. This really isn't a tip but more of a reminder. It's important to allow enough time to familiarize yourself with your equipment. Start shooting early, before the season opener, to become more and more proficient with your muzzleloader. Here are a few exercises that make practice more exciting. I like to have a muzzleloading contest with my friends throughout the summer:

- The distance for the targets and the number of shots you allow are up to you. Personally, I like setting targets up at 50, 100, 150, and 200 yards. Each shooter gets three shots at each distance. I set up a target with two strings at 50 yards, one running vertically and the other horizontally. Try aiming for the point where the strings intersect. When you break the strings, you'll have bragging rights for the rest of the year!
- Hang some crackers by a string at 100 yards and see if the individual who broke the string was just plain lucky or good.
- Hang an empty tuna can up at 150 yards. If you can get a three-shot group, I'd say you're ready for the fall.
- Finally, place a clay rabbit, the kind used in sporting clays, at 200 yards. If you can consistently break the rabbit, you've successfully proved yourself as being proficient with your muzzleloading rifle. After you've gloated for a while with your friends, repeat the contest from the beginning again with no misses.

With the rise of the white-tailed deer population in the United States, more states are expanding the opportunities for the muzzleloading hunter. The technological improvements made in the muzzleloading industry, which are very similar to the archery industry, have also increased muzzleloading hunting opportunities. I am convinced that this sport will continue to thrive in the years to come.

Predators Quiz Answers
(from page 98)

1) True. Wolves are some of America's largest canines and stand taller than humans when standing on their rear legs.

2) d. All of these species feed on plants and animals when the opportunity arises.

3) True. A fox also acts like a cat when it stalks a mouse in a field.

4) False. Males and females work together to care for a litter of pups.

5) d. Timber wolves work in packs to bring down some of North America's biggest game animals. They can use deep snow to their advantage and use their numbers to tag team a deer or moose until it tires of running.

6) b. While the lynx and bobcat are small animals, mountain lions are big animals and have recently been reported in Minnesota and Maine.

7) False. The lynx has the ear tufts.

8) a. *Vulpes vulpes* is the red fox. *Canis lupus* is a coyote.

Bear Quiz Answers
(from pages 102-103)

1) False. Black bear sows normally have two cubs—or sometimes three— every other year. Born hairless and about the size of a squirrel, after a few weeks, the cubs are bigger than a small dog and can climb a tree.

2) d. While most of the black bears in the Southeast are indeed black, in many areas of the Rockies and northern regions black bears can be reddish brown, blond or cinnamon colored.

3) b. The black bear is *ursus americanus*. A grizzly is *ursus horribilis* or the horrible one.

4) True. Bears and most game species are more active during a change in weather—light rain included.

5) b. Black bears breed in the summer, and the sow retains the eggs by delayed implantation before the eggs begin to develop. Cubs are born at the end of winter.

6) False. Black bears are eating machines and will eat grass, berries, carrion, fish, beavers and even other bears when the opportunity presents itself. Black bears also like Twinkies and doughnuts, and hunters use bears' sweet tooth when baiting them.

7) False. Males can normally be recognized for having a short snout and stocky head. Females normally appear to be slender. A lanky bear might be a small young male.

8) b. A male bear is called a boar. Interestingly enough, bears are distant relatives of pigs.

9) a. Partly because they live in a wider range of areas where humans live and visit, black bears have killed the most humans.

10) True. This is an interesting fact about bears. However, if the bear does not have enough food before denning and is underweight, the embryo will be absorbed and no cub will be born.

11) c. Most hunters who are after a rug hunt during the spring when bears are emerging from their dens.

12) d. Polar bears get big by eating, and in a land of limited supply, they are known for eating almost anything they can find. They will wait at a seal's airhole in the ice and grab it when it comes up—or when possble, they'll dive in and swim after a seal. Polar bears are strong swimmers.

Pronghorn Quiz Answers
(from pages 122-124)

1) e. Pronghorns are not related to deer, elk, goats or even the old-world antelope such as impala. Pronghorns developed on the North American plains and are the only living representative of their genus, *Antilocapra*.

2) e. Although some biologists would say "pronghorn" is correct, in most areas of the west "antelope" is the term used; you'll even see that word in some game and fish department publications. "Cabree" is a French-Canadian word meaning "little goat"; this name was given to the pronghorn by the first trappers to see the herds teeming on the northern plains.

3) Trick question. A cheetah could probably beat a pronghorn in a short sprint, but for any distance, a pronghorn could probably beat any animal on earth, and that includes everything out on the African plains. Top speed? That's arguable, but it's probably somewhere around 65 miles per hour.

4) b. Although the bucks begin staging in August, September sees the most frenzied rutting activity.

5) b. Pronghorn bucks prefer to defend a territory and the does that reside there. When pronghorns are disturbed—as they often are by hunting pressure or other encroachments of man—they will defend a mobile harem, but that's much harder work for a buck.

6) False. Pronghorn bucks are among the most vicious of big game fighters and are quite ruthless even when an opponent is down. One Wyoming guide told me about leading a client to two nice bucks who were fighting in a draw. During a lull, the client shot the bigger buck, a nice one. The other buck took the opportunity to gore and stomp the carcass for a few minutes before hunter and guide could get there.

7) a. Pronghorns are browsers (similar to deer), not grazers. Consequently, grasses are not highest on their list of favored forage. Answer "b" could also be considered correct, in some habitats where forbs are easily available.

8) False. Even in deserts, pronghorns need a standing water source. The source doesn't have to be big or fancy, but they need it.

9) b. You will, however, see some bucks in their prime growing into category "c."

10) e. Pronghorns love the wide open spaces where they can see danger coming for miles. Pronghorns—especially bigger bucks—will also go to rough country where most hunters don't venture because the going is a little tough.

11) b. Wyoming is the king of pronghorn states and almost always offers up the most pronghorns to hunters each year. Montana is prime pronghorn country too and comes in a close second.

12) Almost any answer is correct as long as it is a rifle that shoots fairly flatly out to 200 yards—300 if you're really steady—and if you're comfortable shooting at the distance offered.

13) False. Pronghorns evolved without fences and without having to jump over hardly anything. They have not acquired this trait in the relatively few generations of animals that have bred since we plowed and fenced the plains. Although a few will jump fences, they prefer to crawl under and sometimes have trouble doing that. Consequently, fences do restrict pronghorn movement to some degree, and this becomes especially troublesome in winter when the animals may need to move to find forage.

14) False. A pronghorn doe might spend her entire life in a 5,000- or 10,000-acre pasture—not huge by the standards of the endless prairie. Roust a buck from his territory in the morning, and he will probably be back in the afternoon, preferring his familiar haunts over what lies over the hill.

15) c. No question about it. Decoying and stalking are incredibly exciting, but waiting at water in a good blind is the most effective way to arrow an antelope.

16) False. Were it not for the efforts in the early 1900s of a few dedicated hunter/conservationists, we might only have token populations of pronghorn today. Transplanting was common in the 1930s, and the capture technique was pionereed by New Mexico's T. Paul Russell. Think of that name when you witness the grace and beauty of a pronghorn speeding across the sage.

17) False. They're not tired—they're gulping air into their extra-large windpipes.

18) Pronghorns evolved with huge wolves, saber-toothed tigers, cheetah-like cats and other fierce, fast, efficient predators on the plains. During the last ice age, these predators died out, but the adaptable pronghorn survived. Pronghorns still maintain this great speed capability and don't seem to have slowed down.

BIG GAME BIRDS: WILD TURKEY

*I*always wanted to hunt turkeys in another state, but I'd never had the opportunity until this year when I was invited to hunt the Rosebud Indian Reservation near the Black Hills of South Dakota. For months, the only thing on my mind was hearing that monster gobbler strike his note, and thinking about it brought the hair on the back of my neck standing to attention. I left home about 5:00 a.m. and started my ten-hour jaunt across the sandhills of Nebraska and the prairies of South Dakota.

Turkey Heaven

by NAHC Member Rick O'Shea of Centerville, Iowa

I decided that I would try something new, at least for me, on this turkey hunt: I was going to use a muzzleloading rifle, which is legal on the Rosebud Indian Reservation. I'd taken quite a few turkeys with a shotgun but none with a muzzleloading rifle.

I arrived at the camp and was met by my friend Ken and his father. After I unloaded my gear and got settled in the cabin, I sorted out my muzzleloading accessories, filled my speed loaders with two Pyrodex pellets behind a 180-grain Knight Red Hot Bullet and made sure my rifle was still sighted in after my trip. Sure enough, it was still hitting 3 inches high at 50 yards, which would put it dead on at

130 yards. Those turkeys wouldn't stand a chance against my muzzleloader!

We left camp and turned down a road that cut through the open prairie, then we drove past a small pond near a prairie dog town. As I looked closely, one was standing at attention, seeing us off to the timber that graced the skyline. After crossing a gate, we started going up a series of hills to "turkey heaven." When we reached the timber, we parked the truck on an old logging road and thought we would try calling from there.

Ken hit the box call, and immediately we heard a turkey gobble. It sounded close! We looked at each other and decided that this was the spot. We grabbed the decoys and started down the road into "turkey heaven." The weather was perfect—about 45 to 50 degrees with no wind.

Why am I calling this place "turkey heaven?" When we made it to the bottom of the road I saw a small flowing creek with three ridges that came together and a really brushy draw that emptied into a small patch of fresh green grass. It looked like the perfect place to set up to call in a gobbler.

We set up a couple of hen decoys in the grass, and I positioned myself behind a pile of limbs, branches and an old log about 50 yards away from the decoys. Ken and his father were about 40 yards to my right. We let things settle down for a few minutes and then Ken started to call. The hair raised on the back of my neck when I heard that monster tom answer Ken. The gobble was deep, raspy and long. Not only did this bird gobble once, it was double and triple gobbling! Ken tried the call again, and the tom answered along with a couple other birds that sounded like jakes. (They had really shallow, short gobbles.)

I heard some hens yelping behind me, and the tom gobbled again. This time he sounded like he was right on top of us. Given their excellent eyesight, turkeys can really humble even the best hunters so I made sure not to move, fidget or flinch. We waited and nothing happened. The birds did not want to come down into the bottom. Deciding to make a move, we went to the top of the ridge where we had last heard that big tom. Just before we crested the ridge, Ken tried his box call again, and the turkey gobbled not more than 100 yards to our right.

We set the decoys on the side of the ridge and dropped back to some pine trees about 50 yards from the decoys. When Ken called again, that bird gobbled from the brushy draw we had just left. We thought we could beat him to the bottom, so we grabbed the decoys and slipped down to a point that overlooked the logging road by the grassy patch. When we got into position Ken called again, and the bird was back at the top! We were getting very tired of playing these games. We waited about 15 to 20 minutes and heard nothing—not even a gobble or a yelp. When we started to head back to the truck, we heard a hen start calling to the tom. Ken said, "I think we had better sit back down. They're

Then I saw what I had traveled ten hours for: a Merriam!

coming!" I think we learned an important lesson: When turkey hunting, you should stay put, regardless of how tempting it is to move to a better spot.

I got situated, and in about three minutes, a lead hen came down the hill and out of the draw to the green grass. The hen started pecking at the ground, looking for something to eat. We heard some spitting and drumming and knew that the gobbler was getting closer. The next thing I knew, more turkeys were coming down the hill. Then I saw what I had traveled ten hours for: a Merriam! I eased into position and tried to get a shot off, but I didn't have a clear view of the bird. I was going to have to wait for another opportunity. Assuming that the birds were going to take the same path as the hen when they followed her behind the brush pile, I waited and waited, but nothing came down out of the brushy draw.

Out of the corner of my eye, I saw a bright red head coming toward me! First the tom and then two jakes. I raised my muzzleloading rifle and prepared to shoot. The jakes were off to the right by the brush pile, and the tom started to go into full strut, just waiting to make turkey heaven a reality.

I had a clear shot, my aim was steady, I squeezed the trigger and..."BOOM!" The muzzleloader blew smoke.

Turkeys were flying out of the draws, heading for safer ground. I ran to where I had last seen the tom and there he was, lying in the leaves, resting in peace. The tom—which looked like a cross between a Merriam and a Rio Grande—had an 8½-inch beard, ⅝-inch spurs and weighed about 20 pounds. Walking back to the tree where I had set up, I paced off about 13 yards. That's a little close for a blackpowder rifle, but it is a hunt that I will never forget!

Rolling after Turkeys

Missouri holds a special turkey hunt for wheelchair-bound and mobility-impaired hunters. The hunters can use longbows, crossbows or shotguns 20 gauge or larger. Hunters are encouraged to bring hunting partners.

*T*he spring turkey season started out cold and damp and stayed that way most of the season. When we were not fighting the cold, it was the rainy days. And the black gnats were atrocious—even the best insect repellents wouldn't keep them off me.

They were in my ears, under my glasses and biting me like I was a delicious meal. To ward off those pesty gnats—and because I like an occasional cigar—I generally have a pack with me. (I find that the smoke is the only thing that keeps the gnats off.)

Chenango Big Foot

by NAHC Member William Agnew of Guilford, New York

And because turkey hunting is all about patience, patience and more patience, cigars help to pass the time of day. In the three years I have pursued turkeys, I have been fortunate enough to take five. I hunt turkey a little bit differently than most conventional hunters. Normally, I hunt the swamps on state land near my home. I know from lots of time spent sitting in the woods watching the travel routes of the deer and turkeys where they travel and what time of day they use these routes. During these times prior to the turkey season, I sit perfectly still in a field and let them move about without spooking them.

I do not get up early and get into the woods before daylight. I've found that turkeys have a routine each and every day if they're not disturbed. All of my turkeys have been taken between 9:30 a.m. and noon. I know that sometime in this window, the birds will come through the swamp. (I have never tried to call a turkey off its roost.) I generally call about every 30 minutes, using a mouth call or box call when I hear a turkey far off. When I see them or hear them really close, I use my slate call. When I see a tom coming in, I stop calling all together. I've found that this really gets it looking for the hen. At this time, a hen decoy works well. If a tom comes in and doesn't find a hen, it loses interest quickly and gets really wise.

On this particular spring hunt, I had hunted hard on 15 mornings without bagging a turkey. It got very frustrating when on sev-

"It's important to test shot size patterns at a turkey target before the season."

eral other occasions, the flock of turkeys came past my spot in the swamp, but no matter what I did, I could not get a gobbler close enough for a filling shot. I found that it's important both to get a good head and neck shot and to test shot size patterns at a turkey target before the season.

It was getting near the end of the season, and I decided that the next day I'd try some other areas where I had seen turkeys before. On my way home, I drove through other roads in the state forest to do some scouting. As I was driving along, a hen turkey ran across the road in front of my truck. This hen was near a swamp I had hunted before, so I decided to hunt there the next day.

I got into the woods early. It was a really nasty, cold, wet day. I spent the whole morning hunting and did not see anything. I was beginning to think that for the first time in three years I would strike out. I started walking back to my truck on the dirt road and noticed a few deer, raccoon and fox tracks in the mud. Then to my surprise, I saw the foot prints of "Big Foot." They were huge turkey tracks, the biggest I had ever seen. I bent down and broke off a small twig and laid it down alongside the big toe of the tracks. When I got home I measured the twig: it was slightly more than 5½ inches long. Usually anything over 4½ inches is a tom; I knew I had located a big bird.

Over supper that night I told my wife about the Big Foot tracks. I told her that my chances of getting him were slim since it was late in the season, but she and my mother reminded me they had gotten used to the tradition of having wild turkey for Thanksgiving. My wife said, "Get your confidence back, and you can outsmart him."

The next day I returned to Big Foot country. I walked into the woods about 200 yards. When I saw three hens walking through the woods, I immediately ducked down and pulled my camo mask down on my face. I sat with my back against a big tree and saw three more hens. They all disappeared into a small gully where I could not see them anymore. I decided to start calling with my homemade turkey call. I called softly since the turkeys were close and made a series of clucks. Suddenly, a gobbler responded! I readied my shotgun. Up out of the gully came "Big Foot!" I had completely fooled him into thinking I was his soul mate. I waited in silence as the gobbler searched for a hen. When the big tom was 35 yards out, I aimed for its head and neck. When the recoil from the magnum load had cleared, I saw Big Foot flapping around on the ground. I knew he was big but I hadn't known how big until I saw him up close. He was truly the biggest turkey I had ever seen! He had an eight-inch beard and a 5½-inch middle toe. His head was as big as a baseball, and when I picked him up I was really amazed at how heavy he was. (As a retired meat cutter, I've handled a lot of domestic turkeys and am also a fair judge of weight.) I gutted the turkey, filled my tag and headed home. I weighed the turkey on the only scales we had—two different fish scales. Each scale goes to 25 pounds and each registered the 25-pound limit. I figured the turkey weighed at least 28 pounds. Had I preregistered to enter my local sports shop's turkey contest, I would have won.

This turned out to be a great year for me. Chenango Big Foot's mounted wings, tail fan, beard and big feet now adorn my den.

Turkey Hunting Tips

- When hunting turkey on a windy day, call more often so that the birds have a better chance of hearing you.

- On a windy day, position yourself to call in turkeys upwind toward you. In the wind, turkeys prefer to face and move upwind so that the wind is blowing in the same direction as the growth of their feathers.

- During rainy days, place turkey calls in a plastic bread bag to keep them dry. Either operate the calls through the bag or reach into the bag to operate.

- On both rainy and snowy days, turkeys will stay on their roost longer. Look up into tall pine or cedar trees or on a protected side of a mountain when calling turkeys.

Turkey Quiz

See page 188 for the correct answers.

1. True or false? Only male turkeys can distinguish colors and have excellent eyesight.

2. A mature male turkey will have which distinguishing feature(s) that differentiates it from a female?
   a. a beard
   b. spurs
   c. tail feathers
   d. all of the above

3. True or false? A jake is a male turkey with a beard about one foot long, spurs between one and two inches long and middle tail feathers that are slightly longer than the other tail feathers.

4. During the breeding season, male turkeys develop a breast sponge, which is used to:
   a. protect the turkey during predator attacks.
   b. hold fat that will sustain the turkey during breeding season.
   c. alter the pitch of his gobble in order to attract more hens.
   d. all of the above.

5. True or false? A tom is a male turkey with a beard less than four inches long and spurs less than one-half inch long.

6. Baby turkeys are typically called:
   a. toms
   b. cocks
   c. poults
   d. chicks

7. Turkeys will sometimes roll or "dust" in loose dirt in order to
   a. reduce their natural smell and ward off predators.
   b. attract a mate.
   c. rid themselves of insects in their feathers.
   d. turkeys never "dust" themselves.

8. True or false? The best place to shoot a turkey is in the head and neck region.

9. True or false? Wild turkeys rarely fly, and when they do will only glide for a few feet.

10. When male turkeys fight, they may
    a. get into neck wrestling matches.
    b. hit each other with the spurs on the backs of their legs.
    c. both of the above
    d. male turkeys do not fight each other.

Bill Johnson bagged his first gobbler while hunting with Gary Sefton at Alabama's White Oak Plantation.

*I*t was Saturday of the first week of the West Virginia 1997 spring gobbler season. At 11:00 a.m., I got situated in front of a nice-sized pine tree. This looked like a perfect spot, as I sat there on a small knoll overlooking a nice open oak and pine woods.

I based my decision to begin hunting later in the morning on the premise that hens will leave the gobblers by midmorning. This can leave the door open for hunters to call in that lonely gobbler.

A Gobbler Hunt to Remember

by NAHC Member James Barnard
of Middlebourne, West Virginia

I certainly hoped to do that today! There was a lot of sign in the area, so I was confident something could at least hear my calls. I gave a few yelps on a mouth call, followed by a cut on my slate. I let about ten minutes or so go by between each series.

No response. It surely seemed that nothing was close, despite the sign in the area. After almost an hour, I slowly leaned forward to ease some tension in my back. I was well camouflaged and was almost speared by a cardinal as it flew by. I was still wondering what it would be like to get beaked by our state bird when I caught movement to my right.

About five seconds later, I heard what is music to every turkey hunter's ears. Even though I was still leaning forward, I hadn't been spotted. Suddenly, the gobbler appeared and the shot from my Model 1100 found its mark.

I jumped up quickly and hopped over one log, then another. On the second jump, I twisted my left ankle pretty badly. To make matters worse, the bird suddenly took to the air. I was able to anchor the majestic bird with another quick shot, though.

My first gobbler was mine and much appreciated. I lay on the ground and hollered a big "Yee-haw." There was probably a big lump in my throat too. The pain in my ankle was definitely bad and was soon compounded by Mother Nature. Carrying a bird that later was weighed at 20 pounds is not easy while limping badly and being pelted by hail. Yes, hail! It lasted for a good five minutes or more. The best route out was the way I had come in, which was up a small creek hollow. It wasn't an easy route because I had to cross several small branches along the way.

Once I was out of the woods and back to my niece's house, the sun came out. After taking a couple of pictures, I headed home, I got the bird weighed, dressed it out and had my wife take me to the emergency room for an X-ray. Fortunately, my ankle wasn't broken but very badly sprained.

The gobbler had two 9½-inch beards and 1½-inch spurs. This was certainly a day to remember.

Advanced Turkey Quiz

See page 189 for the correct answers.

1. The Latin name for the Eastern wild turkey is:
   a. *Meleagris gallopavo osceola*
   b. *Tukki*
   c. *Meleagris gallopavo silvestris*
   d. none of the above

2. True or false? Generally, female turkeys have longer necks than male turkeys.

3. Male turkeys will shed their beards:
   a. during summer molting
   b. immediately after the spring breeding season
   c. immediately after the fall breeding season
   d. none of the above

4. True or false? Although rarely observed, turkeys can swim.

5. Turkeys were first domesticated in which country?
   a. United States
   b. Mexico
   c. Europe
   d. China

6. True or false? Wild turkeys are very picky eaters and will often pass by a less preferred food source.

7. True or false? Several types of snakes are considered to be predators of the wild turkey.

8. A turkey snood refers to which of the following:
   a. the baggy flesh of skin hanging under the beak and in front of the neck
   b. the gland from which the beard protrudes
   c. the worm-like flesh of skin growing just above the beak
   d. none of the above

9. The wild turkey breeding season is triggered primarily by:
   a. the rise in average daily temperature
   b. a hormonal change brought on by eating early spring plant buds
   c. the increase in daylight hours
   d. both a and b

10. Eastern wild turkeys migrate in winter primarily to:
    a. Mexico
    b. Brazil
    c. Argentina
    d. none of the above

11. True or false? Wild turkeys have an extremely keen sense of smell.

12. Typically, turkeys do not fly because:
    a. their wings are too small to lift their bodies off the ground.
    b. they wear the ends of their feathers off while strutting.
    c. they use running or walking as their primary mode of transportation.
    d. all of the above

I began to worry when I suddenly heard Paul Jacques, North American Hunting Club's Field Test Coordinator, sucking air and slowly gasping for breath. When his breathing switched to full-blown hyperventilating and I could see his legs twitching in spasms, I knew there was real trouble. I glanced in Paul's direction and could see the hen turkey was still standing there feeding about five feet away from him. What was Paul becoming so excited about, I wondered.

Enjoy The Show

by NAHC Staff Member Michael Faw

Suddenly, I shifted my eyes back in front of us and saw three mature Eastern toms in full strut floating our way across the lush spring-green clover field. They were dragging their wings, drumming and parading straight for us. I began to suck air myself and knew exactly how Paul was feeling. I knew if I could hold myself together for a few more minutes a turkey would be in my game bag and I would be a much happier hunter. As I would soon discover, it ended up being easier to wish than to do.

All the action had begun four years earlier when I started applying for a coveted spring turkey tag in Minnesota. I had been unsuccessful at drawing every spring. Paul and I applied together and had planned to hunt together the previous spring. We must have been the only hunters in the state not to draw, or so it seemed. I had talked Paul into applying for a zone near my home since I regularly saw gobblers there. The luck of the draw was not with us, so now during the fourth year, we decided to apply for one of the southern zones. We did draw a tag finally, we were here hunting, and the turkeys were coming to join us.

Finding a zone and drawing a tag is the least of your worries when hunting gobblers in the spring in Minnesota. Apply too early and you could be sitting in three feet of snow and wearing snow camo while hunting. This year, the weather was perfect, and I had plenty of birds located. The proof was there to greet us on opening morning about an hour after the season opened. I guessed I was seconds away from pulling the trigger.

As the gobblers strutted closer, the hen that was beside us began to mosey over to meet the toms. The gobblers stopped coming closer and began to cut figure eights in the field and show their beards to the approaching hen. Three other hens had joined them, and there was a moving mirage-like maze of turkeys before us. I whispered to Paul that when he could shoot a gobbler to let me know and I would shoot at the same time. He whispered back that the hens were shielding the gobbler he had his gun trained on.

Suddenly, Paul whispered that he was ready to shoot. I had to whisper back that now the hens were shielding the gobbler I had my barrel pointed on. The third gobbler stayed at the back of the flock and floated from side to side of the grouping. This gobbler and hen hostage scene went on for ten minutes or more as we strained to be ready when the right moment came. Turkeys were milling around and feeding and staying at the thirty yard line while we waited, and waited and waited.

Just when we knew things were beginning to happen and the birds seemed to be on the move, the hens turned downhill and headed for the edge of the field. The gobblers lined up beside the hens, on the opposite side from us, and went along to accompany the departing hens. When they stopped at the edge of the field, I reached for my call and let out my best seductive cluck. One gob-

Gobblers will sometimes use hens to shield them from hunters, or so it seems!

bler paused to look our way, then it turned and followed the long set of scaly hen legs that had it in such a trance. I had learned early in my hunting career that I can't compete with a long-legged hen, and this proved to reaffirm that lesson.

As the birds stepped out of sight, Paul and I rolled over onto the ground and suddenly began laughing out loud. No one was going to believe this, and we were having a hard time living with what had just happened. At least now we could breathe! We had strived so hard to be gentlemen hunters that we now sat there with unfilled tags, amazed that we had witnessed one of the longest turkey strutting parades I had ever seen. At least we could say we were ethical, and we both agreed it was one of the most memorable hunts of our lives, even though we never fired a gun. We gathered our equipment and headed off to hunt another field.

I hopped a plane later that day to head for another state. After four years, I finally hunted only four hours until my season was finished. Fortunately to save face for us, Paul returned the next morning and bagged a gobbler there in the field shortly after legal shooting hours opened. Oh well, every good hunting story does not end with a shot and a trophy. Sometimes you just have to sit back and enjoy the show!

Aging Spring Toms

Proud hunters often compare the size of their birds, and this can lead to many friendly arguments. But there's another, less tangible question that often puzzles turkey hunters: How old is this bird?

Many myths surround this subject. Some say that any bird over 20 pounds is at least three years old. Others say that a nine-inch beard is a sure sign of at least a four-year-old turkey. Still others claim that a sharp, ¾-inch-long spur indicates a three-year-old bird.

The National Wild Turkey Federation (NWTF) provides some information that seems to settle much of the debate about a turkey's age. First of all, many things can affect the weight of a bird, so weight is not a factor; however, spur and beard lengths are important factors in determining a turkey's age. NWTF provides the following rules of thumb:

Spur Length	Age of Turkey
½ inch or less	one year
½-⅞ inch	two years
⅞-1 inch	three years
1+ inch	4+ years

Beard Length	Age of Turkey
3-5 inches	1 year
6-9 inches	2 years
10+ inches	3+ years

To differentiate between juvenile and adult birds from a distance, look at the tail fan. A bird with longer feathers in the middle of the fan is a juvenile, while uniform length in tail feathers indicates an adult bird. With a harvested bird, you can distinguish adult from juvenile by examining the two outermost primary wing feathers—the longest feathers on the end of the wing. On adult birds, these two primaries will be rounded with white barring that extends to the very end. On juvenile birds, these feathers will be much more pointed and will have no barring near the tip.

Of course, any tom is a prize, and the opportunity to watch and hunt these fascinating birds is one of spring's most exciting outdoor activities.

Source: Kansas Department of Wildlife & Parks

You'll find the following tips about safe turkey hunting, ethical behavior and hunter awareness useful when you're in the field.

1 **Hunt preparation.** Proper handling of firearms is essential for a safe hunt.

2 **Proper clothing.** Hunters should avoid wearing colors associated with wild turkeys such as red, black, white and blue. Wearing red, white and

Ten Suggestions for a Safe Turkey Hunt

by the Oklahoma Department of Conservation

blue, which are colors of a turkey's head, or black, their body color, may confuse other hunters. Wearing blaze orange during the spring wild turkey season is an option worth considering. During the fall, when deer primitive firearms season overlaps with fall wild turkey season, hunters must conspicuously wear either a head covering or an outer garment above the waistline, consisting of daylight fluorescent orange color.

3 **Safety first.** Following these five simple safety rules listed below will help assure a safe hunt.

- Always keep the muzzle of your firearm pointed in a safe direction.

- Treat every firearm as if it were loaded.
- Be sure of your target and what is beyond.
- Know your hunting area and its safe zone of fire.
- If hunting with companions, know their locations.

4 **Hunter awareness.** Most hunters, when hearing a gobbler, try to get as close as possible before calling. However, other hunters may be calling or working the same bird. Don't compete with other hunters. If you're unsure about another hunter's position, stop calling and reassess the situation.

5 **Where to call.** When you are ready to start hunting or calling, sit at the base of a tree that has a trunk wider than your body. This way you can see an approaching hunter, and you are protected from the rear. Use this position to call so you can see in all directions for turkeys or hunters.

6 **Using a decoy.** Safety-conscious hunters are very careful when using a decoy. If you decide to use one, place it so you will be out of the line of fire. Put a tree between you and the decoy. If you are in the open, place the decoy so it faces directly toward or away from you and can be seen by approaching hunters from all directions. Always carry decoys in a bag or backpack while going to and from hunting sites.

7 **Calling.** Your turkey calls may sound like a real turkey to other hunters, so be alert. Don't use calls that imitate a gobbler; experienced turkey hunters believe it's dangerous and unnecessary. Also, electronic calls are illegal in many areas.

8 **Other hunters.** When another hunter approaches you, don't wave your hand as a signal. This movement could trigger a shot. Instead, shout to the other person since there isn't much chance a hunter will mistake your voice.

9 **Identifying your target.** The most critical moment of any turkey hunt is when you decide to pull the trigger. Be absolutely sure the bird you see is a legal turkey. In the "gobbler only" season, this means you must see the bird's beard to identify it as a tom. Never shoot at noise, movement or color.

10 **Leaving the woods.** Once you have bagged your turkey or have decided to quit hunting for the day, unload your firearm. If you have shot a turkey, wrap the bird in camouflage or blaze orange before carrying it through the woods. Walking through the woods wearing a blaze orange vest using the most visible route to your vehicle will also help protect you.

Bountiful Birds

More than 128,000 wild turkeys reside in Kentucky, according to the State's Department of Fish and Wildlife Resources. The state has an annual fall archery-only turkey hunting season.

Turkey Quiz Answers
(from pages 175-176)

1) False. All turkeys can see colors, and they have excellent eyesight. It is often said that a turkey can look into your eyes and determine what you had for breakfast.

2) b. Both species have tail feathers, and every year hunters bag hens with beards.

3) False. Jakes normally have spurs ½ inch long and beards about 4 inches long.

4) b. A tom's breast sponge sustains the gobbler when all he can think about is hens.

5) False. These are the characteristics of a jake or immature gobbler.

6) c. Young poults are very vulnerable to predators and cold weather during their early days of life.

7) c. Turkeys rid themselves of parasites by dusting in loose dirt. They will scratch the soil, lie in the hole and shake around until they are covered with dust. They are pretty comical to watch when they are dusting.

8) True. Turkeys can take a lot of shot in the body and fly away. Head and neck shots sever the spine and can put a turkey down and eventually in your pot.

9) False. Turkeys are great flyers and will take to wing when they want to put a lot of distance between themselves and danger.

10) c. A turkey fight is normally no-holds-barred. Turkeys will intertwine necks, spur each other and flap their wings wildly. You do not want to fight with a wild turkey, and hunters who rush to a downed bird get spurred each spring until the gobbler is completely dead. Beware.

Advanced Turkey Quiz Answers
(from pages 179-180)

1) c. The Eastern turkey is *Meleagris gallpavo silvestris.* Answer (a) is the Osceola turkey, which is similar in color to the Eastern but has a smaller-sized body.

2) False. Females are normally smaller birds.

3) d. Gobblers do not shed beards. The beard grows until the day the turkey dies and is kept short by dragging on the ground while the turkey walks and feeds.

4) True. While they could easily have flown over to the other side, wild turkeys have been seen swimming across big rivers.

5) b. Europeans discovered domestic turkeys in Mexico when they arrived in the new world.

6) False. Wild turkeys have been documented to eat more than 200 items found in the forest and fields of North America.

7) True. Snakes will find a turkey's nest and eat the eggs.

8) c. The snood is the snake-like flesh hanging near a turkey's beak. The wattle is the clump of flesh under its chin at the base of the throat.

9) c. Turkeys are like deer. Daylight affects glands and increases or decreases hormones.

10) d. Turkeys do not migrate. They have a home range that they travel over and feed upon but are unlike many other birds that head south when winter arrives. They stay put and tough the snow out.

11) False. A wild turkey cannot detect odors. One scent manufacturer sold a turkey scent...buyer beware.

12) c. Swift runners, turkeys are quick to dash into the brush.

ESSENTIAL TIPS, LISTS
& OTHER LORE

Technology Leads the Way

by Steve Featherstone

Equipment Essentials

I bet you would love to have a gadget in your pocket that could tell you where you are, where you started from, how to get from one favorite spot to another and, equally important, how to get back to your starting point—a gadget that would do all this at the mere push of a button and with a quick glance. Such a gadget is now readily available...but it is worthless unless you learn how to use it properly.

Hunters, anglers, hikers, birdwatchers and recreational boaters are flocking to the latest technology to ensure they can enjoy outdoor adventures without becoming "temporarily disoriented," or in other words, lost. This technology hides behind the acronym GPS, or Global Positioning System.

GPS is not really a new system. More than 20 years in the making, the Global Position System was developed by the military for precise positioning and navigation guidance, free of the errors, weather interference and various problems of previous systems. GPS works on a network of 24 satellites orbiting about 11,000 miles above the earth and carefully positioned so that at least four satellites are in a direct line of sight at any point on the globe at any time. A simple electronic triangulation of signals to GPS receivers provides an accurate position fix. The devices, which are available to be mounted in a boat or other vehicle—or as a completely portable, handheld device the size of a cell phone— can also calculate distances to a particular location and other valuable information.

GPS units have helped hunters venture into the unknown...and back.

Retail prices for GPS units have dropped steadily. Here are a few tips in purchasing your GPS unit. First, choose a unit that uses replaceable batteries. For greater accuracy than a single channel receiver, choose a unit that contains five or more parallel channels in the receiver. Read the instruction book and practice with the unit until you are completely familiar with it. Finally, be sure you carry and know how to use a map and compass as a fail-safe backup. If batteries go dead or you drop your unit on a hard surface, you will need that map and compass.

Ten tips for using GPS in the outdoors:

1. Don't use GPS for primary navigation. You should always know the land you're hunting on well enough to know when and if you're lost. Basic compass skills are helpful, not only in navigating through the woods but also for understanding how GPS works.

2. A GPS is not a compass. It does not use magnetic fields. Rather, it uses radio signals broadcast from satellites. Unlike a compass, your GPS will work in any weather, can be viewed at night and is not affected by magnetic interference.

3. Depending on how many channels your GPS uses to receive these radio signals, you may need to find a clearing where your GPS can get an open view of the sky in order to calculate your position.

4. Once the unit has locked onto enough satellites (at least four) to get a position fix, you can start navigating. For safety's sake, you should always mark a waypoint where you begin your day's hunt: your truck, your trailhead or the lodge, for example. That way, no matter where you go, the GPS can always point you to the direction from which you started.

5. For obvious reasons, it is advisable not to walk around looking at your GPS while you're hunting. It's best to use the GPS as a backup tool, secondary to your powers of observation and knowledge of the landscape.

6. The best use of a handheld GPS is for marking significant locations or waypoints—a stream crossing, a buck rub, a kill site. Whatever it might be, the GPS will store that location indefinitely and you'll always be able to revisit that exact location.

7. Many GPS units can tell you the exact time of sunrise and sunset in your location, a very important feature for duck hunters or for hunters in states that limit hunting to specific time periods before dusk and dawn.

8. Since GPS uses a worldwide standard of measurement—latitude and longitude—you can exchange coordinates with other hunters to favorite hunting and fishing spots and use your GPS to navigate them.

9. In relatively flat, featureless or scrubby terrain, or on the water, most GPS units will work similarily. When navigating ravines, steep hills or canyons, or when under dense tree cover, the radio signals on which your GPS relies can be blocked.

10. Always carry extra batteries. Even units that have exceptional battery life might unexpectedly go dead. In cold weather, store the GPS near your body to keep the batteries from freezing.

Source: Louisiana Department of Wildlife & Fisheries

Tips for Mounting Scopes

So, you've got a new scope and are itching to get it mounted. Installing a scope on a firearm is an intricate and technically demanding process that can be made easier by following some simple guidelines.

Assuming that you've got the correct bases and rings for the scope, the first step should be to clean all of the screw holes of oil and debris with a quality aerosol degreaser like Shooter's Choice Quick Scrub III. The product not only blows out and displaces foreign agents but also evaporates quickly, leaving you with a clean, dry working environment.

The bases should be secured to the firearms receiver after coating the screw threads with a locking compound such as Loctite. This ensures that the screws will not come loose with recoil. If the bases are ever to be removed, heating the screw heads with a soldering gun will break the hold. The bottom rings should then be loosely fastened to the base and aligned using a one-inch-diameter wooden or aluminum dowel 12 inches long. Place the dowel in the rings (top and bottom) with a piece of 320 grit wet-dry sandpaper wrapped around the dowel. This will uniformly smooth the mounting surface and reduce marring of the scope tube when inserted.

Once the rings are aligned, tighten them to the base, lace the scope in the bottom rings, mate the tops and install the screws firmly but not too tightly. The Shooter's Choice staff of experts suggests for magnum or long-action firearms that the rings be first coated with rubber cement to prevent sliding during recoil.

Next, if you have a collimator (bore sighter), align the scope and bore. If you don't have one, look down the bore to the target and zero the scope to the same target. Before tightening ring screws make sure that the crosshairs are absolutely vertical and, with your cheek flush to the stock comb, move the scope forward or backward in the rings until the field of view is a bright and complete circle. Now tighten all screws alternately to equalize ring pressure.

The scope should now be aligned closely enough to print on a target at 25 yards. Make any individual adjustments at that range until the scope is absolutely zeroed, then make further adjustments at 50 and/or 100 yards.

Source: Shooter's Choice

Good Binoculars Enhance Your Hunting Trip

Outdoor gear. It's an American obsession. Daniel Boone would be dismayed at the huge array of guns, ammo and high-tech accoutrements available to modern hunters. One hunter's basic tool, a pair of binoculars, is still pretty much the same as it has been for 100 years.

Many first-time buyers squander money on inadequate binoculars. Others pay top dollar for good binoculars that are wrong for their needs. With a little information and care in shopping, you can find a pair that fits your hobby and your budget.

Binoculars come in two basic styles: roof prism and porro prism. The optical tubes of roof-prism binoculars are straight, permitting them to fold up into a small package when not in use. This makes roof-prism binoculars the favorite with people who need a lightweight, compact unit.

The front or "objective" lenses of porro-prism binoculars are set farther apart than the rear or "ocular" lenses, making them heavier and more bulky. This disadvantage is offset by the fact that they do a better job of what binoculars do best—providing "binocular" vision.

Humans have depth perception because we have two eyes that are set fairly wide apart. By processing visual information from two different perspectives, we get a better idea of how far away objects are. That's why the images we see through single-tube telescopes look one-dimensional. Binoculars allow us to see more naturally, and porro-prism binoculars enhance that effect by placing our artificial "eyes" far apart in relation to distant objects. If you don't mind the extra weight and bulk, porro is the way to go.

The most basic information is given in a pair of numbers printed right on most binoculars. The first number describes the binocular's ability to magnify distant objects. A 7X35 binocular has a magnification factor of seven times, meaning that objects will appear seven times closer than they do to the naked eye.

Magnification is great, but it has a price. Many novices buy the most powerful binocular they can afford, assuming that making objects appear larger is the same as making them easier to see. They don't realize that a 20X binocular shows an area only about a third as wide as what you would see through a 7X binocular, which makes it harder to locate objects.

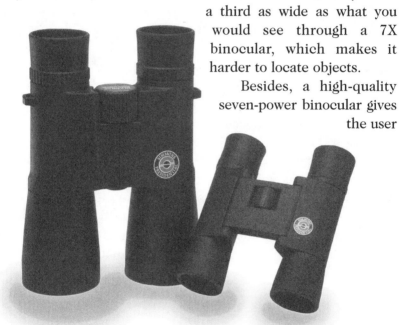

Besides, a high-quality seven-power binocular gives the user a remarkably clear view of most objects, making 20X magnification unnecessary except at a very long distances. In those situations, you're better off with a telescope.

Furthermore, high-powered binoculars cost more, in more ways than one. Besides paying more money, you pay for for magnification in extra weight. A 20-power binocular is great to have occasionally, but the rest of the time, you're just carrying a small millstone around your neck. Big binoculars saddle you with even more than their own considerable weight. With any binocular over about 10X, you have to carry a tripod to hold your big binocular steady enough to see anything without distracting jiggling every time you breathe.

Binoculars in the 6X to 8X range are best for most uses.

The second number printed on a binocular refers to the diameter of the objective lens in millimeters. The objective lens replaces your eye in gathering light. Bigger objective lenses gather more light, providing brighter images that are easier to see.

Many binoculars also bear an inscription that describes their "field of view." In most cases, this will be shown as so many feet or yards at a given distance. This is called "linear" field of view. Some binoculars may be marked with "angular" field of view. A binocular that has an angular field of view of 6 degrees has a linear field of view of 314 feet at 1,000 yards. The wider the field of view, the easier it is to locate an object with binoculars. So, in general, the wider the field of view, the better.

Brightness is the characteristic of binoculars that provides the most fertile ground for misconceptions and advertising malarkey. To put overblown claims in perspective, take the cardboard tubes from two rolls of toilet tissue and tape them side by side. You are now holding the brightest optical instrument on earth. Look through them and you will see all the light that went in the front end coming out the back end. No binocular on the market can equal that performance.

But if bigger lenses gather more light, can't you make the objective lenses big enough to produce an image brighter than what you see with your naked eye? Nope. A 50mm objective lens gathers 100 times more light than the 5mm lens in your eye. But binoculars don't deliver all that light to your eye. Where does the extra light go? Most of it goes to magnification.

To produce a magnified image, binoculars must spread out the light they gather. It's just like the beam of light from a movie projector. The beam is much brighter at the lens, where it is small, than on the screen, where it is magnified.

Some light is lost to optical imperfections in the glass of the lenses and mirrors in the binocular. No optical system transmits 100 percent of light that enters it. Very good binoculars manage only about 90 percent efficiency. Some binoculars are brighter than others, and the differences are apparent when you check them side-by-side.

Another important characteristic of any binocular is its "exit pupil." The exit pupil is the column of light leaving the ocular lens, measured at the point where the light enters the eye. To see the exit pupils, hold a binocular at arm's length, pointing the objective lenses at a bright object. The small round spots visible in the rear or ocular lenses are the exit pupils.

Binoculars come in two basic styles: roof prism and porro prism.

In general, a big exit pupil is better than a small one. Any binocular that produces an exit pupil at least as big as the pupil of the user's eye is positioned precisely behind the center of the ocular lens. However, a larger exit pupil allows the user's eye to stray slightly from the center of optical alignment without losing part of the image.

If you plan to use your binocular in low light, it's best to choose a binocular with an exit pupil of at least 5mm. To calculate the size of the pupil for a binocular, divide the objective lens' diameter by the power of the binocular. For example a 10X50 binocular has an exit pupil of 5mm.

The most common focusing system is the center focusing, with a wheel or lever at the center that focuses both pieces at the same time. Usually one eyepiece (almost always the right), can be adjusted to compensate for differences in activity between the user's eyes. Binoculars made for people who wear eyeglasses usually don't have this adjustment on one ocular. They assume that both eyes are corrected to 20-20 vision.

Some binoculars have individual focusing for each eye. Others are permanently focused at a preset distance that allows the user to see a fairly sharp image from that distance to infinity. Focused binoculars are made for people who don't want any focusing fuss and are willing to put up with third-rate sharpness. Such binoculars are useless inside their minimum focal distance. They are especially unsuitable for birders, who need to see fine details on birds at close distance.

Center-focus binoculars with a separate focus adjustment on one ocular are the best compromise. You have to take time to focus both sides each time you use them, but after that, all you have to do is adjust the center-focus wheel for changes in distance of your subject.

Eye relief, another characteristic of every binocular, measures the distance from the ocular lens to the user's eye. People who wear eyeglasses need binoculars with greater eye relief than those with perfect vision. As mentioned earlier, some binoculars are made especially with eyeglass wearers' needs in mind.

No one binocular is a perfect fit for everyone. Some people's eyes are placed very close together while others' are widely spaced. Almost every binocular allows users to move the two sides closer together or farther apart. But the ocular lenses of some binoculars won't move close enough together or far enough apart for all people to see clearly though both ocular lenses. When choosing a binocular, make sure the ocular adjustment is adequate for your eye spacing.

Similarly, some binoculars are too heavy for everyone to use comfortably. Big binoculars have advantages, but can your hands comfortably reach the focusing controls? Before you put down your money, make sure the weight and dimensions are workable for you.

When you find a binocular you think you would like to own, get two or three others, focus them all on a particular object and then look at it with each binocular in turn. Does your chosen binocular look as clear as the others? Look especially for a rainbow edge on objects—this reveals poor chromatic correction.

Optical glass works by bending light. But glass bends different wavelengths (colors) of light in different amounts. When viewed through a plain glass lens, the different colors of light are split apart like the light coming through a prism. Because the lens splits the light apart, the various colors of light coming from a particular spot strike your eye at slightly different locations. The resulting rainbow effect can be pretty, but it reduces sharpness of the visual image.

Virtually all binoculars have optimal coatings that correct this problem. Cheap ones don't correct it very well. Reject binoculars that show the rainbow effect.

Next, focus your candidate binocular on a flat vertical area at a moderate distance, say the side of a house at 100 yards. When you have it in sharp focus, hold the binocular still and move your eyes to look at the edges of the field of view. Are objects there as sharply focused as those at the center?

Reject any binocular that doesn't give sharp focus throughout the field of view. Otherwise, when an object appears large in your binocular, you won't be able to see it all in focus. Also, blurry peripheral images tell your brain that something is wrong with your eye's focus and your eyes work to correct a problem they can't fix. The result is eye strain and headaches.

Don't waste money on a binocular that always makes you feel as if you're looking through a haze. This will be apparent when you compare the images of several binoculars side by side. Permanent haze makes an image look unsharp, causing the eyestrain problems mentioned earlier.

A separate problem—but one that can look like haze—is internal fogging. If a binocular gets water vapor inside, the moisture can condense on the inside surface of lenses when the binocular gets cold. This should not be confused with external fogging, which can happen to any binocular when the cold glass encounters warm, moist air.

Unfortunately, it is difficult to check for this flaw in a department store. What you can do, however, is check to see if the manufacturer has taken measures to prevent fogging. Binoculars sold as "waterproof" usually have all their openings to the outside sealed with flexible O-rings to provide assurance that water won't get inside to cause fogging. Binoculars sold as "fogproof" usually have been filled with dry nitrogen or other dry gas and then sealed to ensure there is no water vapor inside to cause fogging.

With reasonable care, waterproof, fogproof binoculars will stay that way, but unusually hard rocks can break their seals, leaving them vulnerable to fogging in severe weather. Rubber armored models are more resistant to this hazard.

Some binoculars, especially those with paramount focus, make your eyes do the work of focusing. This and a host of optical imperfections can cause your eyes to strain. Sometimes this strain is subtle, but it is cumulative. After a full day of looking through your binocular, a headache will tell you if you made a bad choice. If you find yourself squinting through binoculars, chances are they aren't for you.

Try this test. Focus the binoculars on an object within 30 feet of you. Make sure that both oculars are in sharp focus. Now close one eye and, using the center-focusing mechanism only, shift the focus to an object near the horizon. Then switch eyes and, without refocusing, check the sharpness of the distant object in the other eyepiece. Both oculars should still be sharp.

Now shift the focus back to the near object. If the binocular has to be readjusted to restore the left-right balance of focus after shifting distances, it means the mechanism that moves the two sides of the binocular aren't sturdy and precise enough to keep them both aligned at the same focal point. It means you will have to fuss with refocusing both eyepieces every time you brush the ocular. Better too tight than too loose.

Armoring protects binoculars from impact when dropped. Loss-proof caps are tethered to the binoculars as an insurance policy for absent-minded users. Other special features abound. You can get binoculars in bright colors that make them easy to find or in camouflage that helps you to be invisible to wildlife. Straps and cases are available to make binoculars easier to carry. Filters can help with special lighting situations.

All these extras have their places, but none of them will make up for basic deficiencies in the areas mentioned earlier. And if you pay attention to all the basics, you're not likely to miss frills.

How much should you pay for a pair of binoculars? The short answer is, "as much as you can afford." You can get sturdy, serviceable binoculars for not much more than $100. But if you are willing to spend more, you will get more...more durability, more precision, more clarity and more brightness. Well-chosen binoculars will do more than any other piece of equipment to enhance your enjoyment of the outdoors.

Source: Missouri Department of Conservation

Tips for Sighting in a Rifle with a Scope

by NAHC Member Kevin Howard

Here are some helpful tips for sighting in a rifle with a scope.

- **Check all mounting screws.** Be sure all the screws on the bases and rings are tight. Some shooters like to use a product called "Loctite" to make sure the screws stay put.
- **Proper scope mounting.** Make sure the scope is mounted straight on the gun and at a comfortable position for eye relief.
- **Adjust focus.** At a known distance, adjust the focus setting of the scope to your eye. This will ensure a clear sight picture.
- **Bore sighting.** Several companies have a bore sighting device that will get your gun close to being on target. Bore sighting can also be done with a bolt action rifle by removing the bolt and looking through the barrel to the target. With the gun in a solid rest, the scope can often be adjusted to within a few inches of being sighted in.
- **Ammo selection.** Choose the brand and bullet weight of the ammo you will hunt with. Different brands of the same bullet weight or different bullet weights of the same brand may have different points of impact.
- **Get a solid rest.** Before you can properly sight in a gun, you must have an absolutely solid rest to shoot from. A range with a bench rest works best, but a picnic table will also work.
- **Sand bags and front rest.** Place the gun on sandbags or in a rifle rest. Make sure to place the forearm of the gun on the front rest; avoid placing just the barrel on the rest.
- **Use proper ear protection.** Hearing damage from loud firearms can be permanent and hurt your hunting skills level.

- **Recoil reducing products.** You may want to use some type of recoil pad or device to reduce the felt recoil.
- **Start at 25 yards.** For your first few shots, start by shooting and adjusting your scope on targets at 25 yards. This will put you close at 100 yards.
- **Decide at what distance you want the rifle sighted in for.** If you are hunting white-tailed deer in the East, you probably want your gun shooting dead on at 100 yards. If you are hunting mule deer out West, your sight-in distance may be 200 or 250 yards depending on the caliber and bullet weight.
- **100 yard adjustments.** Shoot a three-shot group at 100 yards and check your zero. Make adjustments on the scope and allow the rifle barrel to cool. Repeat until the gun is sighted in at the range you want.
- **A spotting scope helps.** A spotting scope helps speed up the process by allowing you to check hits from the bench.

Shoot off a sturdy bench, with sandbags, to make consistent shots and sight-in efficiently and effectively.

- **Take your time.** Enjoy shooting since we can find so very little time to do enough of it in our fast-paced world.

Camo Tips

Here are some camouflage tips that will make you a better hunter:

1. Match the pattern to your surrounding background; consider wearing a different pattern on top and bottom if necessary.

2. Always use camo on your hands and face. These two body parts move more than all others while hunting.

3. Cover anything shiny like your watch, buttons, snaps and zippers. These small details demand great attention.

4. Purchase pants two to three inches longer than needed. This will keep light-color socks and boots from standing out.

5. Wear boots with dark soles. They are sometimes the first thing an animal sees if a hunter is sitting at ground level.

6. Avoid direct sunlight. If possible, face west in the morning and east in the afternoon.

7. Think about your intentions when you pick a spot to sit down or climb a tree. Inside 40 yards, you should concentrate on blending in; past 40 yards, concentrate on breaking up your outline.

8. Set up your stand on edges of cover. Avoid the middle of thick cover, which will hamper your vision and your chances of seeing game, which often travels the edge.

9. Keep your outline as low as possible. Avoid the animal's eye level by crunching down well on the ground or getting 15 feet or higher when using a treestand.

10. Use face paint to touch up around your eyes even if you are wearing a face net to keep down the shine.

11. Don't wear hunting clothes in camp. Hang your camo outside, away from smoke and kitchen smells.

12. When washing your camo, turn it inside out and wash it in cold water with detergent that doesn't contain a brightening agent.

13. Store your camo in a sealed plastic bag during the off-season. You may also want to enclose some pine boughs or cedar.

Fixed Blade
Hunting Knives

Important Features and Benefits to Understand About Hunting Knives

Fixed blade hunting knives are preferred for their strength, their convenience and, to an extent, the romantic appeal of owning man's first tool. While they are used primarily for hunting, fixed blade knives are useful for many tasks, such as:

- cutting rope
- camping chores (e.g., whittling stakes or cutting food)
- skinning or cleaning game

Features of fixed blade hunting knives vary with each manufacturer. Customers may have a different idea of what makes the perfect knife. They are generally interested in one or more of the following characteristics:

- blade shape
- blade length and grind
- steel composition and characteristics
- handle material
- consecution and weight

Blade Shape

Two basic blade shapes to be familiar with are the upswept or clip blade and the drop point.

Hunters who prefer a curved surface for separating hide from the meat use upswept blades. Drop points are preferred by others who say the shape gives them more control and lessens the danger of puncturing the entrails during removal (if entrails are punctured, their contents will fill the carcass, contaminating the meat).

If you are searching for a knife for something other than hunting, consider the task you need to do. Do you need a knife with a sharp point for piercing? Or do you need a stronger point that can hold up to heavy-duty cutting?

Blade Length And Grind

The blade length will depend on the type of task being completed—or your personal preference. If you will be using the knife for small game, such as rabbits or squirrels, a knife with a two- to three-inch blade is generally suitable. For larger game, such as deer, a three- to four-inch blade is recommended. Your preferences, however, may not match the norm.

Hunting knives are flat- or hollow-ground, depending on the manufacturer's design. All can offer good performance if other factors of quality are acceptable.

210

Steel Composition and Characteristics

Most fixed blade hunting knives are made from high-carbon stainless steel. A minority are made from carbon tool steels, which are coated with a chrome finish to prevent unnecessary corrosion. Any product used outdoors or for cleaning game should be cleaned and dried promptly.

Most production knife blades are stamped. Many handmade hunting knives utilize stamped blade blanks. However, handmade knives or more expensive cutlery from Europe might be drop forged. Differences between handmade and production knives can be great or small.

Handle Materials

Handles range from natural materials like wood, leather or stag, to more modern thermoplastics, metal coated with vinyl or resin-infused materials such as Micarta or laminated wood. Natural materials can be visually interesting but may be subject to drying and cracking. Dense tropical woods are not as likely to dry. Manmade materials are often better suited to a product receiving rugged use.

Construction and Weight

Handle materials and blade design significantly affect a hunting knife's heft and balance. Almost all hunting knives have narrow tangs that extend all the way to the end of the handle, offering the optimum in strength, balance and durability. A good handle is mounted securely with rivets or epoxy.

Bolsters may be composed of a variety of materials including brass or nickel silver. A knife with brass bolsters will be heavier than one with a lightweight handle. "Heavier" doesn't mean "good" or "bad," it's just a characteristic. Different people will have different preferences.

Related Products to Suggest with the Purchase of a Fixed Blade Knife

- Sharpening steel
- Crock stick
- Lansky diamond sharpener
- Metal polish

Important Names to Know

- Buck
- Western
- Kershaw
- Parker
- Schrade
- Gerber
- Case
- Puma

Source: W.R. Case and Sons

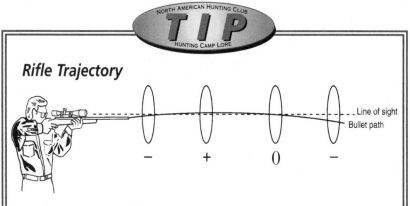

NORTH AMERICAN HUNTING CLUB
T I P
HUNTING CAMP LORE

Rifle Trajectory

Line of sight
Bullet path

–   +   0   –

.22 rimfire, centerfire pistol, shotgun slug and centerfire rifle ammunition all fire a single bullet.

Once the bullet leaves the barrel of the gun, it starts to drop slowly due to gravity. In order to hit a distant target, a bullet must travel in an arched path called trajectory. The bullet will then drop back into the line of sight at some point down range, called zero point, and then continues to drop. While the line of sight remains a straight line to the target, the muzzle must be slightly elevated in order to launch the bullet in an arched path.

Illustration by ZDS

Boot Selection Tips

Nothing can add to your hunting experience, or send you hobbling for camp, as fast as a pair of hunting boots. Here are some pointers to use when purchasing your next pair:

- Try on new boots while wearing the socks you will wear while hunting. It's also a good idea to try them on later in the day or after walking a long distance, so your feet are closer to the size they will be while you walk and hunt.

- Boots that are too tight will restrict circulation and cause your feet to get cold. You can warm your feet by loosening your boot's strings. Proper-fitting boots should allow some toe movement.

- The standard hunting boot height is 8 to 10 inches. This height provides ankle support and protection. Unfortunately, a taller boot can increase the amount of weight you left with your legs and tire you quicker.

- All boots should be worn for at least a week and broken in prior to wearing them on their first hunting trip.

- Your feet perspire more than any other part of your body. Foot powder can help absorb the moisture. To stop a blister, put a layer of moleskin over the area at the first sign of discomfort.

- Even Gore-Tex-lined and waterproof boots will become damp inside if you allow your pant leg to funnel water to the top of the boot. Wear gators!

- Need to know what length of string to buy for your boots? Count the pairs of eyelets, then multiply by eight. For example, eight pairs of eyelets times eight indicates the proper lace length is 64 inches.

Source: Georgia Boots

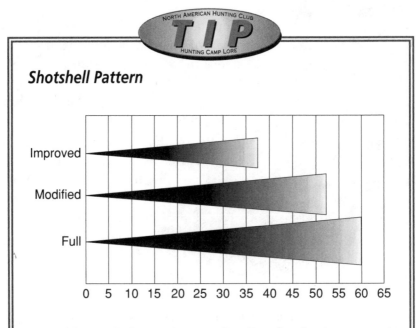

Shotshell Pattern

Most shotgun shells use many small pellets that begin to spread apart after leaving the muzzle. The amount the shot spreads is determined by the choke of the shotgun barrel and the distance the shot has traveled from the muzzle. Choke is a constriction in the end of the barrel. Patterns created by the choke sizes of full, modified, and improved cylinder are illustrated above.

Checklist for Great Photos

from the NAHC Staff

North American Hunter magazine is proud being the only national hunting magazine to publish color photos of members with their game. We use the photos in books like this as well! To continue that tradition, the NAHC editorial staff uses the following criteria to select photos for publication:

Essential Resources

- The photo shows little or no blood.
- The animal's tongue is not hanging out.
- The animal is tastefully positioned—for example, not hanging from a rope or loaded in a pickup.
- No vehicles or buildings appear in the background.
- The photo shows safe handling of firearms, bows, etc.
- No alcohol containers are visible.
- The photo is not a Polaroid.
- The photo shows North American game only (with the exception of fair chase exotics).
- The photo is in focus and properly exposed.

Photos to be considered must be submitted with an index card containing the following information:

1. Member name (If more than one person appears in the photo, please indicate which is the member.)
2. Member number
3. Mailing address
4. Animal taken
5. Location harvested
6. Hunting tools used (e.g., firearm/ammo, bow/broadhead, optics, etc.)
7. Guide/outfitter, if used

Photos are published as space permits, and there is a limit of one photo per member per year. Send your best photo to: NAHC Member Shots, P.O. Box 3401, Minnetonka, MN 55343.

Beautiful deer, tasteful pose, nice shot. NAHC Member Dana Hamby of Hutchinson, Kansas.

Let Your Fingers Do the Hunting

Telephone numbers of organizations that sportsmen frequently contact:

Archery Hotline 800-461-2728. To locate a range, check on a season or find a local dealer.

Bird Banding Laboratory 800-327-BAND. To report the number of migratory waterfowl, 24-hours toll free.

National Wildlife Refuge Locator 800-344-WILD. To find a place to hunt.

National Reloading Manufacturers Association 503-639-9190 (or visit www.reload-nrma.com).

North American Hunting Club 800-922-HUNT (or visit www.huntingclub.com).

Where To Shoot—need help locating a range? Call 203-426-1320 (or visit www.wheretoshoot.org).

Women's Shooting Sports Foundation 719-638-1299.

How Hunters Help Wildlife

Healthy populations of many wildlife species now roam the United States, thanks to something our parents and grandparents did more than 60 years ago. In 1937, Americans agreed to pay a special tax on firearms, ammunition and archery equipment. This created a unique way to protect many different types of wildlife by providing money for the Wildlife Restoration Program. This program, which is administered by the federal government's U.S. Fish and Wildlife Service, makes sure state wildlife agencies can:

- conduct wildlife research and other wildlife management activities
- purchase land that is important to wildlife
- teach the public about wildlife and how to hunt safely and responsibly

As hunters and shooters, we can continue to help wildlife by supporting the Wildlife Restoration Program. Next time you and your friends purchase firearms and ammunition, think of the wildlife you are helping to protect!

How it Started

America is home to an amazing number and variety of wild creatures. But not long ago, wildlife's survival was very much in doubt. The early settlers encountered great numbers of wildlife species, but as the settlers arrived, they changed lands important to the animals' survival. Some wildlife species were wiped out and others were reduced to only a fraction of their original numbers.

Natural and human events also affected wildlife. In the early

1930s, the United States experienced the worst drought and the worst economic depression in its history. Lake beds turned to powder, and dust storms scoured whole regions of the country. Money was scarce for help in wildlife. Animals such as the passenger pigeons were extinct. Bison almost became extinct. In many rural areas, few people remembered seeing species such as white-tailed deer, wild turkey and wood duck.

Then a remarkable thing happened. Hunters and the firearms and ammunition industries joined with state wildlife agencies to create the Federal Aid in Wildlife Restoration Act. The act was signed into law by President Franklin D. Roosevelt September 2, 1937.

Wildlife Restored

Thanks to the Wildlife Restoration Program, wild turkey, white-tailed deer, pronghorn, wood duck, beaver, black bear, the giant Canada goose, American elk, desert bighorn, sheep, bobcat and mountain lion populations have been rebuilt, and their ranges have expanded. Because improved research and protecting important lands help all animals, many creatures that are not hunted—such as bald eagles, sea otters and songbirds—also benefited from the Wildlife Restoration Program.

In addition, millions of Wildlife Restoration Program dollars continue to help states conduct hunter education programs. These programs train 750,000 new hunters in safety and sportsmanship each year. The courses are taught by 55,000 volunteer instructors from all over the United States. Wildlife Restoration Program funds are also used to help build shooting ranges, where you and you family can practice shooting skills for fun and in preparation for hunting.

State wildlife agencies use more than half the Wildlife Restoration Program's money to buy, develop, maintain and operate wildlife management areas. More than 4 million acres—enough to cover all of Connecticut and Rhode Island—have been purchased since the program began, and nearly 40 million acres are managed for wildlife through agreements with other landowners.

Wildlife Restoration Program money also helps wildlife in other ways:

- In the hot and dry Southwest, precious water is caught in concrete "guzzlers," which store rainwater in small, shaded reservoirs for animals. The guzzlers are purchased, installed and maintained using Wildlife Restoration Program money.

- Trees and shrubs are planted in the Great Plains to help pheasants, quail and other wildlife survive winter storms.

- In heavily wooded parts of the Northeast, clearings are created to provide food and shelter for deer, woodcock, rabbits and ruffed grouse. Timber-cutting practices are modified to preserve cover for deer among pines, fir or spruce.

- Livestock grazing in the West is managed carefully to improve habitat for quail, prairie chickens and sage grouse.

- Controlled burning of brush and tall grass in the South stimulates growth of seed-producing plants for wild turkey and quail. Small patches of wildlife foods are planted. Waterfowl habitat is created by cutting level ditches that quickly fill with water and grow plants attractive to ducks. Songbirds, muskrats, raccoons, mink and other marsh species also benefit when these places are created.

The Wildlife Restoration Program is supported completely by firearms and archery enthusiasts. However, the program also helps people who do not hunt. Many of these people watch birds or enjoy nature photography, painting and sketching, and other outdoor activities. State wildlife management areas are also used by hikers and anglers, campers and picnickers.

Everyone benefits from the Wildlife Restoration Program. It is one of the largest and most successful conservation efforts in the entire world. And remember: You are an important part of the program. Every time you and your parents purchase firearms, archery equipment and ammunition, you make America a better place for wildlife.

Source: U.S. Fish & Wildlife Service

Help Bears and Yourself by Following Simple Rules

Utah Department of Natural Resources

When bears and humans come in contact, the bears almost always lose. When bears learn that humans may be a source of food, they often pose a threat to public safety and usually must be relocated or destroyed.

"Unfortunately, because of diminishing available habitat, it's seldom that we can relocate bears," said Boyde Blackwell, mammals program coordinator for the Utah Division of Wildlife Resources. "Most of the available habitat we can relocate bears in is already occupied by other bears and they'll seldom accept a newcomer," Blackwell said. "Other available habitat is often frequented by humans or has been developed for human habitation."

Recently a bear had to be euthanized after getting into food containers left out by campers. This incident, which could have happened in many states, illustrates the importance of following a few simple rules to keep humans and bears safe.

"Most bear problems occur for two reasons," explained Ron Stewart, information and education manager for the Division's Northeastern Region. "The most common are humans attracting bears into a camp with food or garbage. The second reason is someone gets between a mother and her cubs. Both problems usually can be avoided," he advised.

Attracting bears can be intentional or unintentional and involves leaving food or garbage where a bear can find it, Stewart said. "Both are dangerous. Even if you escape unharmed, you may have trained the bear to look to humans for food. The next person may not be so lucky when the bear demands to be fed."

Almost every case of black bears damaging property or attacking people can be traced to someone feeding them or leaving food (including pet food), food scraps and other garbage where bears can get to it, Stewart warned. "Unintentional feeding is especially dangerous because the person usually doesn't know the bear is nearby. Bears have an extremely good sense of smell and can be attracted to camp from miles away. Once inside, they can smell not only the food but also the scent of food that remains on clothing after cooking."

To avoid attracting bears to your camp, Stewart provides the following tips:

- Keep yourself and your camp as clean as possible. Leaving garbage around camp is the most common way of attracting bears. Bears are omnivorous. They will eat anything humans eat, including discarded food scraps. Food wrappers, leftovers, discarded meat, vegetable cuttings and even wash water can attract bears.
- Separate the food area from the sleeping area. This includes not only food and coolers but anything used in food preparation, cooking, eating and cleaning up. All utensils, rags and even clothes used while cooking should be left in the cooking area. If the sleeping area does not have an attracting odor, chances are the bear will leave the sleeper alone.
- When a car or camper is available, store food and garbage inside, in a sealed compartment, such as a trunk. Usually food stored in a trailer or car is safe as long as the windows and doors are closed. Bears are capable of breaking into cars and trailers if they find an opening.
- In the back-country, suspend food, garbage and game 12 or more feet above the ground and between trees that are at least eight feet apart. Even if a bear is attracted, doing so will keep the food out of its reach.
- Bears are also attracted to perfumes, cologne, makeup and especially blood. It is best, whenever you go into the country, to leave perfumes, makeup and deodorants at home. If a bear

wanders into camp, it might be attracted toward the sleeping area by the smell of such products. The smell of blood is an even greater attractant.

While hiking in areas where bears are common, experts recommend making noise by singing or attaching a bell to your pack, Stewart said. The bell and singing alert bears to your presence, and they will move out of your way.

NORTH AMERICAN HUNTING CLUB

T I P

HUNTING CAMP LORE

Proper Tick Removal

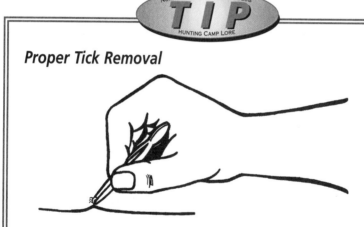

1. Use a fine-point tweezer to grasp the tick at the place of attachment, as close to the skin as possible.

2. Gently pull the tick straight out.

3. Place tick in a small vial labeled with the victim's name, address and the date.

4. Have the tick identified/tested by a lab, your local health department or veterinarian.

5. Wash your hands, disinfect the tweezer, and the bite site.

6. Call your doctor to determine if treatment is warranted.

Source: Lyme Disease Foundation

Illustration by ZDS

10 Tips for Battling Bugs

How to Avoid Bug Bites and
What to Do if You're Bitten

Here are some pointers to help you win the battle of the bugs.

Cover up. Cover your skin as completely as possible. Wear shoes, long sleeves and long pants with the cuffs tucked into socks. Men and boys need to be particularly careful in covering up since males are favored targets of mosquitoes.

Be color conscious. Wear khaki or neutral colors. Mosquitoes are attracted to dark colors, especially blue, so avoid this color.

Use good sense about scents. Heavily scented toiletries are an attraction for bugs and bees. Avoid using scented soaps, lotions and shampoos.

Use repellent. Like sunscreen, insect repellent is an outdoor essential. Apply the proper insect repellent to clothing and any uncovered skin. Products containing DEET and citronella are good choices. Citronella is a natural repellent that rebuffs bugs by confusing their sense of direction and stifling their appetite.

However, be sure to follow the product directions.

- If used with a sunscreen, apply the repellent 30 minutes to one hour after the sunscreen.
- Never use repellents on wounds or irritated skin.
- Wash any residual repellent off the skin when the exposure to insects has passed or when coming indoors.

Be prepared. Always carry repellents in your car's glove compartment or your tackle box, backpack or beach bag. Even the best repellents won't protect you when they are left at home.

Avoid spots popular with bugs. Mosquitoes like cool, moist places. Avoid stagnant pools of water whenever possible. Some popular breeding grounds include puddles, birdbaths and the insides of old tires. Flies tend to to hover around animals and sweets; black flies are attracted to dark, moving objects; hornets nest in trees and bushes; yellow jackets are drawn to food and generally nest in the ground. Bees appear to sting when the weather is gray rather than when the sun is out.

Pick the right time. Be alert to the time of day when certain insects are most active. Black flies are more prevalent in the morning, mosquitoes tend to bite at dawn and twilight, and deer flies are prevalent at midday.

Kid safety. Children are vulnerable to bug bites because they are closer to the ground and to flowers and plants that harbor insects. Make sure they are protected with proper clothing, as described earlier, and with insect repellents that are appropriate to children. If using a repellent with DEET, don't apply it to the hands of children who tend to put their fingers in their mouth. And again, bathe your children when they return indoors for the night to remove any remaining repellent.

Check for bites. Upon returning indoors, check your children and yourself for bites—especially for tick bites. If you find a tick, carefully remove it by grasping its head with tweezers and pulling straight up. To reduce the risk of infection, clean the tick bite with hydrogen peroxide. Be alert for the next 30 days for either a "bull's-eye" rash (a red ring with a white center) at the site of the bite or flu-like symptoms. The presence of either might signify Lyme disease and should prompt a visit to your physician.

Don't scratch. Impetigo, a common disease among children that can spread throughout the whole family, usually begins when a child scratches a bug bite or other small break in the skin. If a bug bite does occur, quickly apply an insect bite treatment such as Tender's After Bite, the top-selling product of its type. Unlike other products that contain lidocaine and benzocaine, which only temporarily mask the itch and can irritate the skin because of their heavy concentrations of alcohol, After Bite actually blocks a bite's effect, thereby discouraging the bite victim from scratching.

For more details, visit the Tender Corporation's web site, www.tendercorp.com.

SHELL SELECTION GUIDE

12	**2¾**	**3¾**	**1¼**	**5**
GAUGE	LENGTH	DR. EQ	OZ. SHOT	SHOT
				SP 12-5

What the Box Tells You

The information above is typical of what appears on a box of shotgun shells. The gauge and the length of the shell are self-explanatory. The piece of information noted as "DR. EQ." is the dram equivalent of the powder charge. This is not the actual weight of the powder, but indicates the approximate velocity that the powder will produce as compared to a standard velocity. The next figure is the total weight of the shot charge in ounces, and the next is the shot size. Larger shot sizes mean smaller pellets. Generally, the larger the individual pellets, the fewer pellets there will be in a given charge.

Negotiating Terrain

Four-wheeling is a wonderful way to see the outdoors and, if done properly, an environmentally sound way to experience the backcountry. Here are a few tips to help you negotiate the terrain and enjoy your four-wheeling experience while protecting the environment.

Off-Road Essentials

• Put your vehicle in four-wheel drive before you reach any hills, obstacles, large rocks, soft spots, ravines ruts and stream crossings. Generally, low-range transfer gear is best for most off-highway use.

• Because you will be on an upward surface, it's especially important to avoid sudden acceleration, sudden turns or sudden braking. Any of these actions could cause the vehicle's center of gravity to shift and destabilize the vehicle, leading to a collision or rollover.

Hills

• Driving safely up, down or over hills requires excellent judgment and an understanding of what your vehicle can and cannot do. If you have any doubt about you or your vehicle's ability, don't drive up or down that hill; turn around and find another route. Re-tracking is a normal part of safe off-roading.

• Travel straight up or down a hill or grade. Don't climb at an angle, or cross the face of a hill below the top. You may slide sideways, or even roll your vehicle.

• Use low gear in the transmission and transfer case.

Obstacles

• Cross obstacles at an angle, one wheel at a time. This raises the clearance of the vehicle.

• Don't cross the obstacle straight on or you may get undercarriage damage at the rear since the rear overhang is generally greater and you may get high-centered.

Large Rocks

• Carefully put a tire on the rock. Proceed very slowly in low/low, with just enough throttle to maintain headway. This raises the vehicle, adding clearance to the undercarriage.

• Don't straddle the rock. This may leave you high-centered on the frame or differential, and damage the frame and/or driveline.

• Know where the low points on your vehicle are (the rock grabbers) the differentials, transmission, transfer case, etc.

• Know what size obstacles your vehicle can clear.

• Use a "spotter" in front of your vehicle to let you know what is going on underneath the vehicle.

Soft Spots (Mud, Soft or Loose Soils, Sand)

• Avoid mud if you can while remaining on the road or trail. If you can't, use low gearing and just enough throttle to maintain forward movement.

• Engage locking differential or hubs. If necessary, winch yourself through.

• Turn the steering wheel rapidly from side-to-side if you sense a loss of traction. This can help generate additional traction.

• Don't gun the engine. This will spin the tires and dig you

DOWN, not forward, and could bury you to the frame. Smooth, easy power is better than too much power.

Crossing Ravines

• Turn into ravines, large depressions or "whoop-t-dos" at about a 45-degree angle, left or right (turning into, not away from, the depression), and let the vehicle enter and leave one tire at a time.

• Go slowly, allowing the vehicle to stabilize itself.

• Don't enter straight into a depression. You may wedge yourself in front first or hang up the front and rear as you attempt to exit.

• Know your approach and departure angles.

Dealing With Ruts, Gullies and Trail Washouts

• Straddle ruts, even if they are wider than your vehicle. This may mean running your tires on their sidewalls along the inside of the rut. This will keep your vehicle level.

• It is important to keep your vehicle level while maintaining control. Be patient and go slowly to keep your vehicle balanced front-to-back and side-to-side.

• If you feel the vehicle tilt, turn into the direction of the tilt and gently apply more power. As it levels out, return your steering back to the direction you want to go.

• Don't spin your wheels. You may dig in, get hung up, slide or roll your vehicle.

Crossing Streams

• Cross slowly, at a 90-degree angle to the stream, or at a slight angle to minimize stream bed damage. Crossing slowly also helps keep water out of the engine's air intake. Create a steady "bow wake" that will form an "air pocket" in and around the engine bay and away from tires if water is bumper height.

• Don't charge across the stream, creating spray and rooster tails. Think of stream crossing in boater's terms: Make them "No Wake" areas.

• Don't drive up and down the stream bed. It disturbs fish and other aquatic habitat.

• Cross streams only at trail fording points. Check the water depth. If it is higher than your engine's air intake, don't cross. Water in the engine will stall it.

• Check your brakes after water crossings.

> HINT—Here's a quick depth guideline for stream fording. Hub depth or less: generally you should have no problems. Hub to bumper: Check air intake height and proceed slowly. Bumper to bottom of headlights: Use extreme caution; sudden dips in the stream bed could mean water in the air intake. At headlights or above: Do not attempt, generally at or above the air intake. Regardless, the best advice is to follow the guidelines in your owner's manual since all vehicles are different.

Turning Around

• Don't try to turn around on a narrow road or trail, unstable ground or steep hillside. You may slide off the road or trail or roll the vehicle. Back up until there is a safe area to turn around.

• Back straight down a hill or steep incline, using reverse and transfer case "low" range.

• Stay in gear, keeping your foot off the clutch and throttle.

Apply the brake gently ("feathering the brake") to keep from locking up the wheels, which may cause a skid.

• Keep your foot off the throttle. This allows engine compression to assist in braking.

• Keep all four tires rolling. This will help control your vehicle.

Guiding

• Use guides for safety whenever possible. They can see things that you can't, especially when backing. Assign only one person to guide. Guide from in front of a backing vehicle or stay well behind. Guide from the uphill side of a vehicle or stay well downhill.

> HINT—When guiding, locate the lowest point on the vehicle and give instructions to avoid hitting. Give clear and concise instructions verbally and by using hand signals.

If You Stall

Here are some tips to get your truck on track again should you stall in the back country.

Automatic transmission: Apply the foot and emergency brakes, then put the transmission in PARK. Start the engine, and with your foot still firmly on the brake, put the transmission in low or reverse. Release the emergency brake, then slowly release the foot brake until the vehicle begins to move. Then gently apply throttle.

Manual transmission: Don't depress the clutch. Keep vehicle in gear and engage the starter. The combination of low range and first gear or reverse will allow the engine to fire and move at the same time. If you stall again, repeat. This procedure allows you to maintain full control. You won't damage the starter, and it preserves your clutch.

If you have a late-model vehicle with an ignition lockout, do the following: Set the emergency brake. With your left foot, depress the clutch and with your right foot, depress the brake. Shift into first or reverse (the transfer case in low), and start the engine. Keep your foot on the brake, and gradually release the clutch until you feel it engage. Release the emergency brake and the foot brake until the vehicle begins to move. Then gently apply throttle to maintain forward momentum

Keep Your Distance

- Keep a safe distance between vehicles. Enter tough spots one vehicle at a time. A vehicle on the other side of the problem area may be able to help you by serving as a winch point or for towing.

- Wait for the vehicle in front of you to make it successfully to the top of a hill before proceeding. The driver may be unable to make it and will need to come back down.

- Keep the vehicle behind you in view to make sure it doesn't encounter any problems.

- Don't tailgate. The vehicle in front of you may stop suddenly, back up or even begin to slide backward.

Reconnoiter Ahead on Foot. When In Doubt, Get Out!

- Know what's ahead of you. Even if you know the trail, stop frequently, get out and walk ahead and observe. Leave nothing for granted.

- Know what difficulties are ahead before you encounter them. Evaluate the alternatives and find the easiest, least dangerous and least damaging choice.

- Don't barge on regardless! Besides, getting out and walking ahead lets you enjoy the surroundings, and refreshes you for the challenges ahead.

tread lightly!®

LEAVING A GOOD IMPRESSION

The Tread Lightly! Vehicle Checklist

Planning for any backcountry journey requires proper preparation. Whether it's a week or a day trip, your vehicle needs to be in top condition. Here's a checklist of critical vehicle components to help assure a safe and trouble-free trip.

Cooling System

☐ Check for leaks, cracked or bulging upper and lower radiator hoses and heater hoses.

☐ Check for radiator leaks.

☐ Check the radiator antifreeze level and condition. Replace or top off to proper level.

☐ Check thermostat and radiator cap for proper operation.

Suspension

☐ Check suspension, steering bushing. Replace cracked, worn or damaged bushings.

☐ Check steering linkage and box for looseness. Tighten or replace weak components.

☐ Lubricate steering linkage and suspension components requiring lubrication.

☐ Check for soft or leaking shocks.

☐ Springs should be properly seated. Check for weak, sagging or cracked springs.

☐ Check spring shackles for wear, proper location, tightness. Locate to proper position; tighten if necessary. Replace worn shackles.

☐ Check alignment. Realign all four wheels if necessary.

☐ Check wheel bearing. Replace bearing if worn. Tighten properly. Repack with grease.

Engine

☐ Clean engine and check for oil leaks. Repair or replace gaskets or seals.

☐ Change oil and filter if needed.

☐ Change dirty air filter.

☐ Clean carburetor or fuel injectors. Check idle; adjust. On carburetor engines, check float for proper operation and height. Adjust to correct setting.

☐ Check throttle return springs. Replace weak springs.

☐ Check fuel pump for proper fuel pressure.

☐ Check fuel pump, lines, tank, carburetor/injection system for leaks.

☐ Check spark plugs. Replace or reset to correct gap.

☐ Check plug wires, coil, distributor cap, rotor, points, ignition timing. Replace worn or damaged parts. Adjust timing.

☐ Check PVC valve.

☐ Check for vacuum leaks. Repair or replace faulty hoses.

☐ Check accessory belts, alternator, water pump, power steering pump, air conditioner. Tighten or replace if worn or frayed.

Brakes

☐ Check drums and/or rotors. Have turned or replaced if outside of tolerances.

☐ Check pads and/or shoes.

☐ Check brake fluid levels. Bring to proper levels.

☐ Check for cracked or checked brake line hoses, line conditions, fluid leaks. Replace worn, leaking or excessively rusty components.

☐ Bleed brakes.

Driveline

☐ Check for leaks in transmission, transfer case, differentials.

☐ Check fluid levels in transmission, transfer case, differentials.

☐ Check universal joints and CV joints. Lubricate if necessary.

☐ Check all skid plates. Tighten loose bolts. If critical areas aren't protected, install plates.

☐ Check wheel bearing. Tighten properly. Repack if necessary.

Exhaust System

☐ Examine condition of muffler and tailpipes. Replace if excessively rusty, leaking or noisy.

☐ Check hangers; the muffler and exhaust pipes should be well above the lower level of the frame. If broken or weak, replace. Tighten loose hangers.

☐ Check protective shield beneath catalytic converter. Replace if loose, broken or missing. The catalytic converter gets very hot, and without protection can set dry grass on fire. Also ensure that no grass or other vegetation has collected on the plate. Consider skid plate protection for both converter and muffler.

Wheels/Tires

☐ Check wheels for damage, especially along the rim. Straighten if possible or replace.

☐ Check tire pressure. Repair leaks. Inflate tires to proper level. Check balance of wheel/tire.

☐ Replace excessively worn tires.

☐ Use valve caps.

☐ Check condition of spare wheels and tires. It's a good idea to have more than one, just in case.

Electrical System

☐ Check battery condition. Clean terminals, seal with dielectric grease. Have voltage and amperage capacity of battery checked. If low, replace the battery.

☐ Check output of alternator.

☐ Examine wiring. Check for worn or melted insulation, shorts, blown fuses. Check condition of plugs and terminals. Make sure grounding straps and terminals are clean, and the proper ground is being maintained. Repair or replace. Spray entire electrical system with a waterproofing material.

☐ Check headlights, auxiliary lights. Aim the lights properly, and be certain each is functioning properly.

☐ Check taillights and turn signals. Replace failed bulbs.

Other

☐ Check wiper blades. Fill windshield washer reservoir.

☐ Check power steering pump and lines for leaks. Check fluid level.

☐ Remove anything on the winch or its support accessories that may cut or gouge into trees, the ground or limit ground clearance.

Having your vehicle in top operating condition will help avoid problems on the trail and will help protect the environment.

tread lightly!®
LEAVING A GOOD IMPRESSION

Ammunition Answers for Hunters

Select a caliber and bullet design to match the prey you will pursue. The following calibers will be good for varmints such as crows, prairie dogs, groundhogs, foxes and coyotes.

.22-250 Remington	.25-06 Remington
.223 Remington	.257 Roberts
.243 Winchester	.270 Winchester
6mm Remington	

The following calibers are recommended for light, thin-skinned game such as pronghorns, mule deer, whitetails and black bear.

.223 Remington	.30-06 Springfield
.243 Winchester	.300 Winchester Magnum
6mm Remington	.300 Savage
.25-06 Remington	.308 Winchester
.257 Roberts	.32 Winchester Special
.270 Winchester	.356 Winchester
7mm Remington Magnum	.375 Winchester
.30-30 Winchester	

The following calibers offer delayed, controlled expansion for big game with tough skin and heavy muscle and bone such as elk, moose and brown bear.

.270 Winchester	.338 Winchester Magnum
7mm Remington Magnum	.356 Winchester
.30-06 Springfield	.375 H & H Magnum
.300 Winchester Magnum	.458 Winchester Magnum
.308 Winchester	

Source: Winchester/Olin Corporation

Deer Calling Tips

by NAHC Member Gary Sefton
of Franklin, Tennessee

Calling Essentials
- **Deer**
- **Turkey**

Most deer hunters use calling as an effective method of attracting deer without considering why deer calls work. White-tailed deer are social animals. They spend the majority of their lives in loosely formed groups usually consisting of family members and others of the same sex. In order to maintain cohesion and consistency within the group, deer use a combination of vocalizations and body language to communicate with each other. They use variations of three sounds—the snort, the grunt and the bleat—in varying degrees of volume and intensity to communicate their most basic emotions: "I'm afraid, I'm lost, back off, come here," and so on. Deer respond to these sounds for a variety of reasons, the most basic being: social, curiosity, territorial or dominance infringement and mating anticipation. Keeping these basic facts in mind, the following tips and techniques can help you become a more effective deer caller.

Calling like a deer. Your first priority in becoming an effective deer caller should be to learn the language! This should be a rule, a mandate, a commandment. Most deer hunters own and use deer calls. Ninety-eight percent of deer hunters who use deer calls have no idea what they are saying when they blow on their call; they're just making a noise and hoping something shows up. You can move a step ahead of other hunters by doing some research on deer vocalizations (an excellent reference video titled "Real Vocal Whitetail" is available from Woods Wise Products) so that you know what to say, when to say it, and what it should sound like.

Calling in the early season. Deer respond to calls in late summer and early fall out of "social curiosity." They are interested in other deer in their immediate area and will come to investigate. Social curiosity is a sex-specific response, meaning bucks are interested in other bucks and does are interested in other does. Make buck sounds to call bucks and doe sounds to call does. To arouse a buck's social curiosity, try the "attention grunt," a short, soft monotone grunt that means, loosely translated, "I'm over here, everything is all right, come on over." To call early season does, use doe "attention grunts" or lost contact doe bleats.

Pre-rut calling. Pre-rut—the two or three weeks prior to the peak of rutting activity—is the best time to call a buck deer. Bucks are in the best physical condition they've been in all year, maximum levels of testosterone are coursing through their veins and few, if any, does are receptive. When bucks are as active as they are during this time, any calling technique can be effective. Doe bleats will trigger a mating anticipation response, and buck grunts can elicit social curiosity or dominance (territorial) infringement activity—the same with antler rattling, sniff wheezes and aggravated grunts. Check with the DNR in your area for dates when the majority of the does are bred, and count back three weeks from that date. That's prime calling time.

Calling during the rut. Mating anticipation is the response you can anticipate during the rut. Most of us do our hunting in areas with a huge imbalance in the doe-to-buck ration. When you have anywhere from 9 to 15 does for every breeding age buck, there is no competition for the does. Using buck grunts and horn rattling in this situation is usually non-productive. Bucks are not looking for other bucks but they are looking for receptive does. Doe bleats are music to a buck's ears when his mind is on romance, as are the urgent bleat-bawl sounds made by a "breeding bellow" type call. The peak of the rut can be a tough time to call since you have to catch a buck when he's between does. If you catch him when he's looking for a doe and you can sound like a doe you're going to get to see him up close.

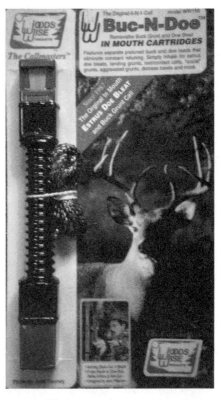

Post-rut calling. After the rut may be the hardest time

Deer calls can produce results when used properly.

to call bucks since they are locked into an almost desperate survival mode that doesn't include much social interaction. Physically depleted, some bucks have lost as much as 25 percent of their body weight and won't be aggressive about anything. However, bucks still have the desire to breed does, so doe bleats may be effective during this time.

Using fawn bleats. If you want to have some fun with a deer call, try a fawn bleat call in September or early October. Make terror-stricken distress cries (which sound like a baby crying) on the call as loud as you can for as long as you can. Does respond to this call dramatically. Some of the does you call to won't respond, but those that do will come charging in with their ears laid back, their hair standing up and fire in their eyes. The closer you get to the rut, the less likely does are to respond to a fawn bleat because does disassociate with their fawns during the rut (for the fawn's protection) and actually avoid fawn sounds.

Antler rattling. As previously discussed, antler rattling during the rut in a high doe-to-buck ratio area is usually non-productive. Try using light sparring and horn tickling sequences in the early season. Bucks start sparring as soon as they shed their velvet and will respond to these sparring sequences out of social curiosity. Continue the sparring sequences until the bucks start actively chasing the does, then switch to the doe sounds.

Setting up to call. I do most of my calling from a tree and try to position myself so that the first time I see the deer, it is within range. Be sure to pay special attention to wind direction when setting up to call. If you call from an open area, the deer will approach up to a point where it thinks it should be able to see the deer it heard, and then it hangs up. Not getting the visual reinforcement to the audible signals it has been receiving, the deer becomes confused. My favorite calling setups are in thick areas with just a few shooting lanes. Deer responses to calling are conditioned responses; everytime a buck has heard a doe bleat and has gone to investigate, it has found a doe. When it hears a doe bleat then gets your scent, a buck will definitely not come in. Additionally, you've weakened the conditioned response chip so that the next time that buck hears a doe bleat, it's not going to be sure what made the sound. A three- or four-year-old buck will retreat if it isn't sure about something.

How often should you call? The best way to attract a deer to your call is to sound like a deer. Deer don't call a lot in social situations, and they never make sounds for no reason. If you hear a deer grunt, either there's another deer close by or it is responding to your calling. For early season calling, use the social sounds sparingly—one or two soft grunts every five to ten minutes. Sounds that portray urgency—such as lost contact bleats or estrus bleats-may be repeated often, but I use them in five to six bleat sequences to give deer a chance to respond.

How loudly should you call? The passive, conversational

sounds deer use to communicate socially are not very loud. If you were 40 yards away from a buck, you probably wouldn't hear its "attention" grunt without excellent hearing and the expectation of hearing it. Keep this in mind when you try to elicit a social curiosity response. Any loud sound you hear a deer make is either an alarm sound, an aggressive sound or a frustrated sound.

When you see a deer. The hardest deer to call is usually a deer you can see. When you see a deer, it is either leaving something, going to something or where it wants to be. Deer usually have an agenda and are single-minded about pursuing it. That is not to say you shouldn't call to a deer that you see; if you know what to say and when to say it, you won't run the animal away. At any time of the year, I start out with estrus doe bleats when I call to a buck that I can see. Because it's the most direct and incautious response, I want a mating anticipation response when I can get it. If the bleats don't work, I try some "attention" grunts. Watch the deer closely as you call to it. Even when it doesn't respond, it will often acknowledge the calling with some form of subtle body language (like an ear flick or a tail wag). Never call to a deer that is coming toward you; just let it come. If you try to rush it, the deer will look you right in the eye and the game will be over.

What about aggressive calling? During the peak of the pre-rut period, aggressive calling can be effective; however, when—and if—deer do respond to aggressive calling, they tend to go downwind to scent-check the situation before they commit to their approach. They will usually respond just as well—and with less caution—to the less aggressive social sounds.

Do deer calls really work? Every year, I talk to people all over the country about calling deer. There seems to be a common occurrence among hunters when they call up their first deer: The deer almost always gets away! Because the hunter often isn't ready when the deer responds to the call, the deer is able to escape. Don't make the same mistake! When you use a deer call, expect to see a deer and be ready!

While you don't have to use a deer call to be an effective deer hunter, calling adds a dimension to your capabilities that can mean the difference between success and failure. Calling allows you to alter a situation that would otherwise be beyond your control: You can stop a deer, move a deer or cause the deer to change its course to your advantage. In order to be an effective deer caller, you need to call up one deer. I don't mean just stopping the deer; I'm talking about jerking it around by the neck like it's on a string; I mean being able to see in its eyes as the deer approaches that it's looking for whatever made that sound.

Woods Wise Call Master and NAHC Member Greg Sefton called in and arrowed this buck while bowhunting in Illinois.

Once you acquire that confidence factor, you'll be a deer caller from that day on.

There are no magic bullets and no deer calls made by elves. The only trick to calling anything is knowing what to say and when to say it. Learn the language. Make the right sounds at the right time, and you will call some deer.

Turkey Calling Tips

by NAHC Member Gary Sefton
of Franklin, Tennessee

If you are a hunter and haven't tried turkey hunting, you owe it to yourself to give it a try; it will most likely change your life. The following tips on calling and hunting will help get you started in the right direction. Wild turkeys have a large vocabulary in comparison to other birds. More than 20 significant vocalizations occur in turkeys' communications among themselves. By learning what these sounds mean and fashioning instruments to reproduce these sounds, we can effectively attract turkeys with artificial calling.

Calling like a turkey. If you hope to communicate with wild turkeys on their level, you'll need to learn their language! Devoting some time to research and practice with your call will help you become a successful turkey hunter. Audiotapes featuring actual turkey sounds are invaluable as learning aids. The best of the bunch—Lovett Williams's "Real Turkeys" series—includes biological explanations of each sound. Woods Wise's "Vocal Turkeys" video features not only the actual turkeys but also graphically detailed instructions on reproducing sounds on a variety of calling instruments.

Calling in the spring season. The most effective sound to use to attract a gobbler in the spring is the hen "yelp." Although the "gobble" gets more publicity, the yelp is the signature sound of the wild turkey. Made by both sexes, the yelp is a two-syllable, two-note call consisting of a high "kee" sound that is slurred into a lower pitched "youk," resulting in a "kee-youk" sound. Yelps—depending on the volume, sequence and intensity of their delivery—can send a variety of messages. The most important yelp

245

sequence for a spring gobbler hunter is the "plain yelp," which is a series of evenly spaced yelps (five or six) that don't vary much in volumes or intensity. Since the plain yelp is often made in the presence of other turkeys—excluding it from the "lost yelp" category—its precise meaning has puzzled biologists. If nothing else, the plain yelp says, "I'm a hen turkey and I'm right here," and it will make an old tom strut and gobble in the spring. If everything else is in place the turkey will come to investigate the source of the yelping.

Basic turkey vocabulary. The other yelp variations—lost yelps, assembly yelps, tree yelps—are better heard than read about because some of the tone and inflection variations are too subtle to describe accurately. Cutts, cackles, putts and clucks are other turkey vocalizations you should be familiar with and will eventually want to add to your calling arsenal as you become more comfortable with the language. If you're just starting out, concentrate on the yelps. Most turkeys that are called with any of the other sounds could have been called with yelps.

Setting up to call. Almost as important as calling is knowing how and where to set up to call. Always try to set up against a tree large enough to break up your outline. If you are right-handed, face a little to the right of where you think the turkey will appear—vice versa for lefties. Setting up just off center increases the area you can cover with your shotgun. You cannot wear too much camo and you can't sit too still! (How to set up is the easy part; sitting still is an ongoing challenge.)

The most common mistakes turkey hunters make are the result of setting up in the wrong place. Two places will always be wrong: setting up too close to the turkey so it can see you and setting up in an open area that allows a turkey to scrutinize your position before it comes within shotgun range. Setting up too close usually happens after roosting a bird the night before. Thinking you know where the turkey is, you sneak in before first light, set up and wait for daylight. When you hear him drumming, he's close—too close! You can't move or call or even think about calling. If you can sit still and not move or twitch for the next 30 minutes—or until the turkey decides to fly down—you might be able to work the bird when it gets on the ground, but it usually goes the other direction. As long as there is some kind of a screen or barrier to block its view of my position, I like to get as close as possible. (Hint: When you're deer hunting from a treestand, you have a "turkey's-eye view" of the surrounding landscape.Keep that in mind when you set up on a gobbler in a tree.)

When calling to a turkey on the ground, always try to set up so that the first time you see the bird, it's within easy shotgun range! If it can see your position from 75 or 100 yards out, a tom will expect to see the hen it has been responding to. It hears the hen but can't see it and becomes confused. You now have a classic "hang-up" situation. Set up within 30 yards of a rise or a bend or some kind of physical obstacle the turkey has to negotiate before it can make visual contact. Make the turkey look for you!

Try calling just loud enough for the turkey to hear you.

When and how often should you call? There is no chiseled in stone answer to this question, but there are some basic guidelines you can hang your hat on until you come up with your own formula. Call whenever you want to initiate a response from a gobbler. Once it responds, come right back with another call. See if the bird is serious or just gobbling out of courtesy. If it gobbles back at the next call, respond to it every time it gobbles until the turkey gets so cranked up that it cuts off your calling sequences with its gobbles. When it's wound up so tight that it can't blink its eyes, quit calling! I mean stop! Let him soak. If you're set up right and have the patience and self-discipline to abstain from any kind of calling, most of the time that turkey will walk into shotgun range. If a hen won't go to a tom, the tom will go to the hen. It may take a while—depending on how far away the tom is to begin with—and there will be times when you think the turkey has left the country, but after a good dose of the silent treatment it should start making ground. And if the tom is any kind of a sport, it will gobble from time to time so you can mark its progress. If it gobbles and is plainly going the other way, then you should try to crank it up again.

How loudly should you call? Since you are trying to communicate with a totally different species in their language, you will always have some nagging doubts about your calling. Volume-wise, the rule of thumb is to try calling just loud enough for the turkey to hear you. If it continues to respond, you're at the right volume. For close-in confidence calling, call softly, just loud enough for a person to hear it at 25 or 30 yards. When you are trying to locate turkeys with turkey calls, start out softly, and if nothing answers, increase the volume to as loud as you can get. Don't worry about being too loud from a distance. You can hear a hen yelping a half mile away on a good day.

Choosing a turkey call. There are hundreds of different styles of turkey calling devices, but they can all be lumped into two main categories: those operated by air and those operated by friction. They are all designed to reproduce the yelp of a hen turkey.

Box calls, slates and push-button calls fall into the friction category since the sound is produced by rubbing two different surfaces together. Box calls are among the oldest of call designs and have been around forever. Box calls are easy to use and make great hen yelps by simply shuffling a hinged lid back and forth across the rim of a box. A good box call should come pre-tuned, so it should never be sanded; however, an oil-free chalk—such as carpenter's or railroad chalk—should be applied to the lid as needed. Box calls can be noisy. To keep them from squeaking and squawking while you walk, place a large rubber band around the call. You can also place the call inside a bread bag or a large plastic bag during wet weather.

Push-button calls are ingenious spring-loaded devices that

produce excellent hen yelps by the simple push of a button. If you can fog up a mirror, you can yelp on a push-button call. Measures must be taken to silence push-button calls while you're walking, and they too can be placed in a bag during rainy weather.

Slate and glass friction calls—or peg-and-pot calls—are my personal favorites because I believe they are the most accurate of all calls. They are easy to use: For easy, accurate hen yelps, simply stroke the surface of the call in small circles with the peg, or "striker," holding the striker much as you would a pencil with the eraser angled away from your body. A variety of different calling surfaces are available, from slate to glass to aluminum. Each surface has some distinct characteristics, and, depending on the acoustic design of the instrument, each can sound like a turkey. The Woods Wise Alumatone makes an excellent call that features all three surfaces. I'm hard to fool when I hear a man using a box or diaphragm call, but I have a hard time telling the difference between a turkey and a good slate-caller. Glass and aluminum are waterproof when played with an acrylic or carbon striker. Slate and wood strikers tend to absorb moisture and won't function when wet. (Hint: Keep a butane lighter with you in your turkey vest; when the rain stops you can use the lighter to dry the striker and the slate surface.)

Diaphragm calls, wing bone calls and tube or snuff can calls fall into the air-operated category. Both wing bone and tube calls can be effective in the hands of experienced callers, but both are hard to master. Diaphragm calls, the most versatile of the air calls, are probably the most popular because they are inexpensive and not that hard to master. If you've used diaphragms without success, try placing the call in your mouth with the horseshoe facing out, then hiss like a snake. (This forces the air column to originate from your diaphragm.) Once you can make a sound on the call, increase your tongue pressure until you make a high-pitched whistle. The whistle is the first half of the yelp. Try saying a word like "cut" or "choke" while making the high note. Voicing either one of these words will force you to drop your jaw. Diaphragm calls take some practice and dedication but they are worth the effort.

Locating a turkey. Before you call to a turkey, you need to know where it is. Locating a gobbling turkey takes top priority when you enter the turkey woods, and there are several ways to make a turkey gobble and reveal his whereabouts. I place them in two categories: non-turkey sounds that trigger a "shock" gobble, which is an involuntary response, and turkey sounds that elicit biological responses such as mating anticipation or territorial infringement, which are communicative responses. The shock gobble is the one you want, when you get it. When a turkey shock gobbles, it isn't aware of its own reaction. Shock gobbles are involuntary, and turkeys don't pay any more attention to them than you would a sneeze. When a bird responds to a turkey sound, it is alert and aware of the fact that it isn't alone in the woods and its attention is focused on your location. Shock the turkey if you can.

A variety of locator calls are specifically designed to shock turkeys. Barred owl hooters and crow calls are the traditional shockers, and they work well, especially at first light. After fly-down time, the tom is strutting its stuff for the hens. While it is single-minded in its pursuit of the hens, only something special will jar a gobble out of the tom. That's when you need some "power noise." Thunder, sonic booms, train wrecks, ambulance sirens and other loud and abrupt noises will make a tom gobble when it doesn't want to. I call it stimulation overload. The "Screamin' Peacock" call by Woods Wise is designed to produce the stimulation overload response, and it's a lot more reliable than thunder and train wrecks. If you can make a gobbler give away its location without revealing your own, you have a foot in the door.

Conclusion

I can tell you how to set up, how to locate turkeys, how to call and how to cook a gobbler, but the turkey itself will ultimately be the one to teach you how to hunt. Find a call that you have some confidence in, and get out there with the turkeys. Hunt safely!

Index

M

N

O

P

Q

R